AF010948

DRAGON HUNTING!

FAMILY WALKS WITH DRAGONS

IN NORTH EAST ENGLAND
AND THE SCOTTISH BORDERS

DRAGON HUNTING!
FAMILY WALKS WITH DRAGONS
IN NORTH EAST ENGLAND AND THE SCOTTISH BORDERS

Stuart Miller

© Stuart Miller, 2022

All Rights Reserved. No part of this publication may be reproduced, stored in a retrieval system, or transmitted in any form or by any means – electronic, mechanical, photocopying, recording, or otherwise – without prior written permission from the publisher or a licence permitting restricted copying issued by the Copyright Licensing Agency, 90 Tottenham Court Road, London W1P 0LA. This book may not be lent, resold, hired out or otherwise disposed of by trade in any form of binding or cover other than that in which it is published, without the prior consent of the publisher.

Moral Rights: The author has asserted his moral right to be identified as the Author of this Work.

Published by Sigma Leisure – an imprint of Sigma Press, Stobart House, Pontyclerc, Penybanc Road, Ammanford, Carmarthenshire SA18 3HP.

British Library Cataloguing in Publication Data
A CIP record for this book is available from the British Library.

ISBN: 978-1-910758-53-3

Typesetting and Design by: Sigma Press, Ammanford.

Cover photograph: © Stuart Miller

Photographs: © Stuart Miller

Maps: © Sigma Press

Printed by: Akcent Media

Illustrations: © Debbie Shawe

Disclaimer: the information in this book is given in good faith and is believed to be correct at the time of publication. No responsibility is accepted by either the author or publisher for errors or omissions, or for any loss or injury however caused. Only you can judge your own fitness, competence and experience. Do not rely solely on sketch maps for navigation: we strongly recommend the use of appropriate Ordnance Survey (or equivalent) maps.

CONTENTS

Acknowledgements	7
Introduction	11
The Walks	
1. Bamburgh and Fowberry (9.5 miles or 6 miles)	19
2. Netherwitton and Longwitton (6.5 miles or 6 miles)	33
3. Penshaw Hill and Cox Green (6 miles or 5 miles)	45
4. Neasham and Sockburn (8 miles)	58
5. Hutton Rudby and Sexhow (5.5 miles)	69
6. Liverton and Handale (6 miles)	78
7. Nunnington and Stonegrave (7 miles or 4.25 miles)	89
8. Hovingham and Slingsby (6.5 miles)	100
9. Renwick and Haresceugh (3.5 miles)	110
10. Morebattle and Kale Water (4.5 miles)	121
Recommended Reading	133

ACKNOWLEDGEMENTS

My thanks are due to Jane Evans and Sigma for their work on this book. They are also due to my grand-daughter Rosie Callaghan who was very much my muse when it came to dragon stories!

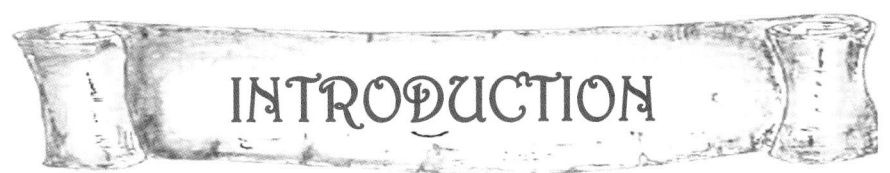

INTRODUCTION

Of all of the British dragon stories the one which is the most famous is *The Lambton Worm* which was much popularized in the form of a Victorian music hall song. However there are very many dragon or 'worm' stories throughout Britain. This book of walks focuses upon ten such stories in the north east of England and southern Scotland. For each of them the format consists of an outline of the story, comments upon origin and 'evidence' and a guide to a walk around the area associated with the legend. Only one of the walks, the Linton Worm, does not cover the ground immediately associated with the story but it is no more than a couple of miles from Linton Church and affords excellent views from a hillside of the relevant area. That is also, by the way, the only walk of the ten which involves any hill walking.

Although the walk instructions in this book are detailed and the walks have all been followed at least twice to check them out you should take with you the appropriate Ordnance Survey map, although the sketch maps associated with each walk should give you enough information to follow the route from point-to-point. In the guidance notes relating to each walk the title(s) of the relevant maps are given. You should always be aware that physical changes can be made which may affect the route instructions eg. a stile may become a wicket gate, a right-of-way may have been diverted. Also be aware that stiles in particular can be a problem for those who are not so nimble footed, and often the problem stiles are indicated in the instructions. By and large there are no significant gradients to overcome although the Linton Worm walk in the Morebattle area does involve some moderate hill climbing. The terrain can be very muddy in places and may be badly overgrown in the growing season so you should be clothed and shod appropriately.

Along the banks of the River Wear (the Lambton Worm) there is Giant Hogweed growing in places. This is a dangerous plant and should not be touched because this can trigger of intense rashes on the skin and extreme sensitivity to sunlight. The main riverside path, though, is kept clear and is fenced in many places so you should not expect to encounter the plant normally.

THE STORIES

All of the stories are based on original accounts which date back many centuries, although the earliest full printed versions tend to be found in 19th century antiquarian collections. In all cases there is an accepted standard format but different versions will display embellishments – good stories, after all, do improve with the retelling of them over time. It is clear that the stories have much in common with each other but beyond that they do have their own characters and colouring. The accounts given here are the basic accounts but with occasional 'improvements'! The Renwick Cockatrice and the Linton Worm are light on detail in the older versions so they have been somewhat filled out albeit in 'tasteful' ways which are in keeping with the main plot.

As regards terminology you should note the following. The word 'worm' is used in this context to mean 'vermin', which is the original derivation of 'worm'. Thus any dangerous and threatening creature such as a wild boar or wolf could be accounted as vermin or 'worms'. The stories related in this book all date from very early times and are clearly about dragon-like creatures. Dragons were/are an amalgam of creature formats. They combine bat-like wings with scaly, serpentine bodies and the talons or claws of birds of prey. Observers usually agree also upon their amazing regenerative ability which meant they could regrow lost limbs and body segments. Their main weapons are their ferocious fangs and their poisonous and fiery breath, although in some of these stories you will encounter additional imaginative features.

There are various types of dragon as well. The heraldic five-door hatchback Welsh-style dragon is the most recognized one. However many medieval depictions of dragons show more modest standard two-legged wyverns. The griffin, benevolent bringer of good fortune and treasure, has the head of a hawk but the body of a lion. Then there are the vicious and poisonous cockatrices which are smaller and bat-like and far less common. There are only a couple of cockatrice stories in Britain but one of them is based in Renwick near Alston and Melmerby.

WHAT YOU WILL NEED TO TAKE

Most of these walks should be easily completed in three or four hours without any great effort. However one person's 'leisurely stroll' can be another person's long distance nightmare so you should always walk within your capacity and that of your companions. You should always wear proper boots or walking shoes and carry plenty to drink, especially in hot, dragon-hunting weather, and food of course if you intend to eat on the walk – dragon hunting

What you will need to take...

- Proper boots or walking shoes ☐
- Lots of drink ☐
- Food for energy ☐
- Waterproof clothing ☐
- Pencils and paper ☐

Warning!!
Do NOT wear RED!
Don't Forget a Mirror!

is a hunger-making business. In all cases there is information about inns or eating places on the routes or which are very near. Carry waterproof clothing as well because the weather can change quickly.

Also carry with you a pencil(s) and writing pad(s). Associated with each of these walks is a simple quiz, wordsearch etc. Dragon hunting can be such a wearing activity as you trudge the highways and byways while parents work out the route and admire views and so on. Children need something to wile away the hours. Apart from trying the quizzes a few good drawings of dragons and suchlike blue-tacked on the kitchen wall would be a worthwhile memory of a day of exploration.

Now as far as the dragons are concerned a few words of advice may be suggested.

Avoid wearing anything obtrusively red because cockatrices are driven demented and furious by the sight of the colour and will descend on you without further provocation. Do carry a mirror though because cockatrices (or basilisks) can turn their victims to stone with a glance and a quickly produced mirror can turn the tables easily. Somewhere about your person carry an iron edged or pointed weapon. It must be made of iron though because, according to legend, only iron will kill dragons. There is some debate about the weaker points of dragons to go for – if you get close enough of course. Some enthusiasts suggest the eyes but others would recommend a thrust in the less protected throat area. *How To Train Your Dragon* is a bit too optimistic I fear. These are dangerous, unpredictable and aggressive creatures. A piece of rowan wood would be handy as well. The wood of the humble rowan or mountain ash tree has magical powers and can provide a barrier against witchcraft and spells (and toothache incidentally). Full armour is, as always, optional.

Horses are a luxury but good dogs know their job and should be given scope as long as you are not crossing land where livestock roam and where they should be on leads. It is unlikely that you will possess an ichneuman, the medieval name for the mongoose. When it sees a dragon, the ichneumon covers itself with mud and,, closing its nostrils with its tail, attacks and kills the dragon. In reality the mongoose does attack snakes and is so fast and protected by its dense coat of fur that it is usually successful.

As far as children are concerned these are worth taking with you for two reasons.

They can scout out the land ahead of you. Younger eyes can detect dragon movement much more quickly, and being more nimble and fleeter footed children can alert the main party to such dangers. Also if you do have to run to escape at any point you can always discard children behind you to delay pursuing dragons – after all they delight in 'swallying bairns' as a standard part of their diet. The youngest and smallest first of course.

THE DRAGON

Now a few words about the nature of dragons and the origin of dragon stories. The word 'dragon' has been interpreted widely in this book to include dragons, wyverns and – in one case – a cockatrice. You will meet no griffins which, incidentally, have nests of pure gold at the bottom of the end of a rainbow. In fact the transmission of dragon stories is easier to explain than the origin of them.

Dragons seem to have entered Europe from Asia via the Roman province of Dacia (mostly modern-day Rumania). Impressed by the dragon images used on Dacian tribal standards the adaptable Romans began to use dragon headed standards for their cavalry units. Cleverly these were designed in such a way that as cavalry charged the wind blew through the open mouth of the dragon head and through a sort of 'wind sock' and produced a frightening noise – which might work well against ignorant savages like the 'nasty little Brits' (as the northern British tribesmen are described in a letter at Vindolanda).

From Rome the image will have easily spread throughout the Empire. A couple of clear relationships here are the Anglo-Saxon and Norse invaders of Britain in the period from the 5th century to the 11th century. The Roman army was very much open to merit and easily absorbed the talents of peoples who were conquered or lived on the borders. Angles, Saxons and Scandinavians all served in Roman or Byzantine army units – the most famous of which was the Varangian Guard of the Byzantine Army. The dragon was a commonly used image – most obviously on Viking *Snekkja* longships. This will, perhaps, explain why by far the greatest number of dragon-related stories in Britain lie within the area most associated with Roman control and Anglo-Saxon penetration rather than the Cymric or British areas of Wales, Cumbria, Southern Scotland and South West England. On the other hand dragons do feature in British lore and poetry. Of course it is in *Beowulf*, the most famous of Anglo-Saxon sagas, that an especially famous and terrible dragon dwells.

The story of Saint George and the Dragon (and the virgin) is probably the most famous dragon legend and is associated with the Age of the Crusades. As a warrior St. George was popular with soldiers and this period can be regarded as the second wave in the influx of dragons into British folklore. If a date can be given to many of the dragon stories of Britain it seems to be around the 13th to 14th centuries.

So much for the transmission of dragon stories. The actual origin of the concept of dragons is a great deal more difficult to deal with. Animals such as the Komodo Dragon, the *draco* flying dragon lizard and the basilisk lizard can be dismissed as 'dragons' since they were named after the fabulous creatures rather than being the originators. Equally the idea that dragons are somehow a folk memory of dinosaurs is unlikely since there were no humans on earth at the time of dinosaurs. It is feasible though, that the discovery of the skeletal remains of dinosaurs reinforced the concept.

Dragon images and dragon stories are found all over the world and in the earliest human traditions although the arch-typical dragon is the Asiatic model. Dragons are a sort of compilation of elements drawn from a variety of fearsome animal types, with the features of crocodiles, serpents and birds of prey all added together. Strangely though, the dragons of the Eastern tradition are benevolent creatures which play a positive role in community events while the dragons of the West are awful and malign monsters. They are two-sided.

One other aspect is worth noting and that is that many, perhaps not all, dragon legends have water in common in some form or other. Rivers and lakes often feature in the terrain associated with the dragons, and often play a crucial role. It is argued that this lies at the heart of dragon mythology and may explain the double edged character of the dragon. One line of explanation may be to do with the need to propitiate the heavens and to impel the rains and the rising of rivers which produced the fertility of the soil which was so vital to the survival of communities – and possibly by sacrifice to achieve this. In that case, of course, one would need to sacrifice not creatures or humans who were near the end of life and useless but those who were young and fertile.

So fortified by your awareness of the origin and transmission of dragon stories enjoy walking with dragons!

WALK 1
BAMBURGH AND FOWBERRY

A wicked and jealous stepmother, a princess turned dragon and three kisses by a wandering knight are the basis of this imaginative story. That, and the most spectacular castle in Britain, easy woodland and field paths and an idyllic coastal stretch make up this journey into a magical kingdom.

THE LAIDLEY WORM

The great castle at Bamburgh which stands on the impressive basalt outcrop and dominates the village below is only one of a number of great fortresses which have crowned the summit. The curious story of the Laidley Worm dates from a period long before the existing castle stood there.

There was once a king living in Bamburgh who was known for his kindness and fairness to his people. He married and had two children – a boy known as Childe Wynd and a daughter called Margaret. Sadly his beautiful wife, the queen of Bamburgh, died and he was left a widower to bring up his children. The son, when of age, went away to seek his fortune abroad as a soldier. Margaret remained though, to serve as the mistress of Bamburgh. She was a beautiful and graceful young woman, slender, fair haired and blue eyed. She was much loved by the people of the area, who saw her mother in her ways and features.

One day though, as the king was out riding, he came across a woman who entranced him and made him forget his dead wife. She had raven-black hair, eyes as black as the sloe berry and skin as white as the petals of blackthorn. He was soon captivated by her looks and by her queenly ways. Indeed he took her for his wife.

The old king and his new queen returned to Bamburgh in a great procession which was welcomed by throngs of villagers who admired her beauty. Yet she noticed that when the king's daughter Margaret was observed to come from the castle to meet her father and his new queen and hand over the keys the shouts of joy from the assembled villagers were far greater than those for herself. She could hear one of the courtiers in the bridal procession say softly to his neighbour that while the queen was indeed beautiful her beauty was eclipsed by that of the princess. From that moment she was deeply jealous of Margaret, and this jealousy was to fester and darken over the coming months.

Then one day the princess disappeared. The people of Bamburgh and the courtiers were grief stricken, and searched throughout the land for her. Nowhere could she be found. After some time it was agreed that Margaret must have drowned in the sea while walking on the rocks near the castle. Now the queen ruled Bamburgh and controlled her besotted old husband.

Indeed only the queen knew that Margaret had been transformed by her witchcraft into a great serpent-like dragon which haunted the woods around the Spindlestone Crags. The spell she cast was of these words:

> *"I weird ye to be a Laidly Worm,*
> *And borrowed shall ye never be,*
> *Until Childe Wynd, the King's own son*
> *Come to the Heugh and thrice kiss thee;*
> *Until the world comes to an end,*
> *Borrowed shall ye never be."*

Of course she meant that the girl would never be freed from the curse since it was unimaginable that she could be saved in such a way!

The dragon grew and grew. As it grew it became ever more dangerous and devastated the land around Bamburgh. No person or animal was safe from the talons and fiery breath of the monster. Even the witch had no spell of strength enough to harm this loathsome worm which was of her making. The kingdom was faced with ruin. In fact so far did news of the dragon spread that the Childe Wynd heard of it, and he decided to return to try and save his father's subjects and rescue his own inheritance from the menace. So he crossed the sea to the shores of Northumberland.

However the evil queen heard of his approach, and feared that if he landed and sought out the dragon he might learn that it was the result of her own evil doing. So as his ship approached the shore she conjured up storms to prevent him, and the wild winds and heavy seas forced him to retire. In fact three times he tried and three times she prevented him from landing.

The adventuresome youth recognized that the storms were the result of witchcraft and could only be counteracted by magic of a similar strength. In fact he had learnt much while he was away from his home land and he did know of the strength of the magic rowan tree. The bark and berries of the humble rowan tree are a well-known antidote for witchcraft and a cure for numerous illnesses. So the Childe Wynd had his crew rebuild his vessel from the wood of rowan trees, the ropes were remade from the rowan bark and the sails were dyed from the juice of rowan berries. And thus fortified the Childe tried one more time. The witch summoned the help of spectres once more and conjured up a storm which was even greater than before. However this time the ship was able to sail into Budle Bay near Bamburgh, and to land at Waren Ford at the head of the bay.

The prince leapt from his ship and ran across the sands. He took horse into the deep and dark woods around Spindlestone. There, near the cave in which it took refuge, he met the dragon which reared up above him and seemed poised to kill him and devour him. He raised his sword to slice at the serpent and then was amazed to hear the beast speak.

The dragon said to him:

> "O quit thy sword and bend thy bow,
> And give me kisses three,
> For though I am a poisonous worm,
> No hurt I'll do to thee"

Childe Wynd was astonished at these words and when he looked at the awful features of the creature he could not bring himself to do as it asked. Yet when he looked into its eyes he saw kindness and great pity. Putting down his sword on a rock he reached forward and kissed the dragon once, twice and then three times. And before his eyes the awful beast seemed to dissolve and be reborn in the shape of his sister, Margaret.

She wept tears of joy at being restored to her proper state by her brother and at meeting him after so many years. She told him of all that had passed since he left Bamburgh and they resolved to return to the castle to free the land and their

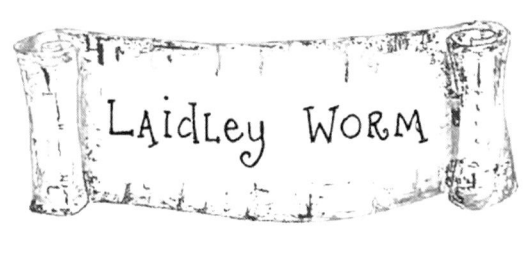

LAIDLEY WORM

father from the magical powers of the witch-queen. So they rode back to the castle astride the horse of the prince. There they confronted her in the great hall before the assembled courtiers. When she saw them she grew pale and afraid because she knew that strong as was her magic she had met her match at last.

The Childe Wynd determined that she should suffer in a way which had been inflicted by her upon his sister. He pointed at her and he invoked his own magical powers with the words: "Now you yourself for a punishment for your many evil deeds shall be turned into an ugly toad". As he pointed and as he spoke her beauty and form dissolved into that of a toad – which was then hurled down the well in Bamburgh Castle.

And there she remains until this day....

NOTES
Even by the standards of dragon stories it must be admitted that this one is especially imaginative – and somewhat questionable regarding family relationships!

The story has had many retellings and redrafts although the basics remain the same. The physical and geographical features associated with it are real enough. Bamburgh Castle is no illusion. There has been some sort of fortress on the outcrop since the 5th century and Bamburgh for many years was the capital of the kingdom of the great realm of Northumbria which was once the greatest of the Saxon kingdoms. Late medieval British author Thomas Malory identified Bamburgh Castle with Joyous Gard, the mythical castle home of Sir Launcelot in Arthurian legend. The present castle was heavily and too enthusiastically restored in the 19th century by Lord Armstrong of Cragside (the 'Great Gunmaker') who owned it. The cottages built for the large labour force employed are still standing to the south.

Budle Bay is a beautiful inlet where the families of local tourists and caravanners play in the soft sands. The head of the inlet is Waren Ford where the prince landed to accomplish his deed – after coffee and biscuits at the Warren House Country Hotel possibly! There is a Spindlestone Crag which is named from a curious rock feature supposed to resemble a spindle. Apparently there were caves once upon a time but the crag has been subjected to quarrying. Very close to the Crag, and overlooked by a caravan park, is the so-called Laidley

The well in Bamburgh Castle is 100 feet deep and cut through solid rock

Pool where the Loathsome (or Laidley) Worm used to bask. Indeed it is marked on Ordnance Survey maps as the Laidley Pool. Inside the castle keep is the deep well which was sunk through solid basalt rock – and there dwells the toad/witch/ queen. Fortunately it is blocked at the top to prevent sightseers trying to peer down and fall in!

The story is claimed to date from as far back as the 13th century although the earliest printed version is 1812. It has a lot in common with a famous Icelandic saga about two children of a jarl. One of them is Hjálmpér whose evil stepmother commands him to work as a thrall (or slave) until he has performed an impossible task. The curious element about the kissing of the loathsome worm may be linked to a story of Sir Gawain of the Round Table who turns a woman beautiful by agreeing to love her.

The Victorian artist Walter Crane was so taken by the story that he painted a version of it *The Laidley Worm of Spindleton Heugh* in 1881. Crane recorded the origin thus:

"In the summer of 1877 we went to Bamborough with our two young children – I think on the recommendation of Mr. Howard (future Earl of Carlisle), who had shown me some admirable studies he made there. I found plenty of subjects, and, among others, Spindleton Heugh gave me in its curious legend of The Laidley Worm associated with the spot, materials for a romantic picture, which I afterwards carried out and exhibited at the Grosvenor."

THE WALK

What you need to know	
Distance	9.5 miles for the full circular walk or 6 miles for the abbreviated version
Time	5 hours for the full version or 3.5 hours for the short version
Map	OS Explorer 340 Holy Island and Bamburgh
Starting point	Car parking (free) along the roadside on the B1342 west of Waren Mill overlooking the Lindisfarne-Budle Bay National Nature Reserve. Grid Reference NU149345

Terrain	Mostly tracks, footpaths and field edges. Some road walking. A couple of short steep gradients. It can be very muddy and overgrown in some sections
How to get there	From the A1 follow the B1342 to Bamburgh. Postcode for SatNav: NE70 7EE (Waren Mill)
Refreshments	Various inns and restaurants in Bamburgh

1. From the parking area turn right towards Waren Mill then left along a lane near the Warren House Hotel. It winds right and left then enters woodland. At a footpath sign on the left (Drawkiln Hill) turn left through trees uphill. The path levels out then you go through a wicket gate and follow the left edge of a field. Note the substantial lime kiln on the right. Go through another wicket gate and keep on to go through a wide field gate. Now head left towards a field corner and trees. Spindlestone Heugh towers above on the left. Go through another wide gate and keep on past a caravan site.

Spindlestone Heugh. The Childe Wynd encountered the Laidley worm here

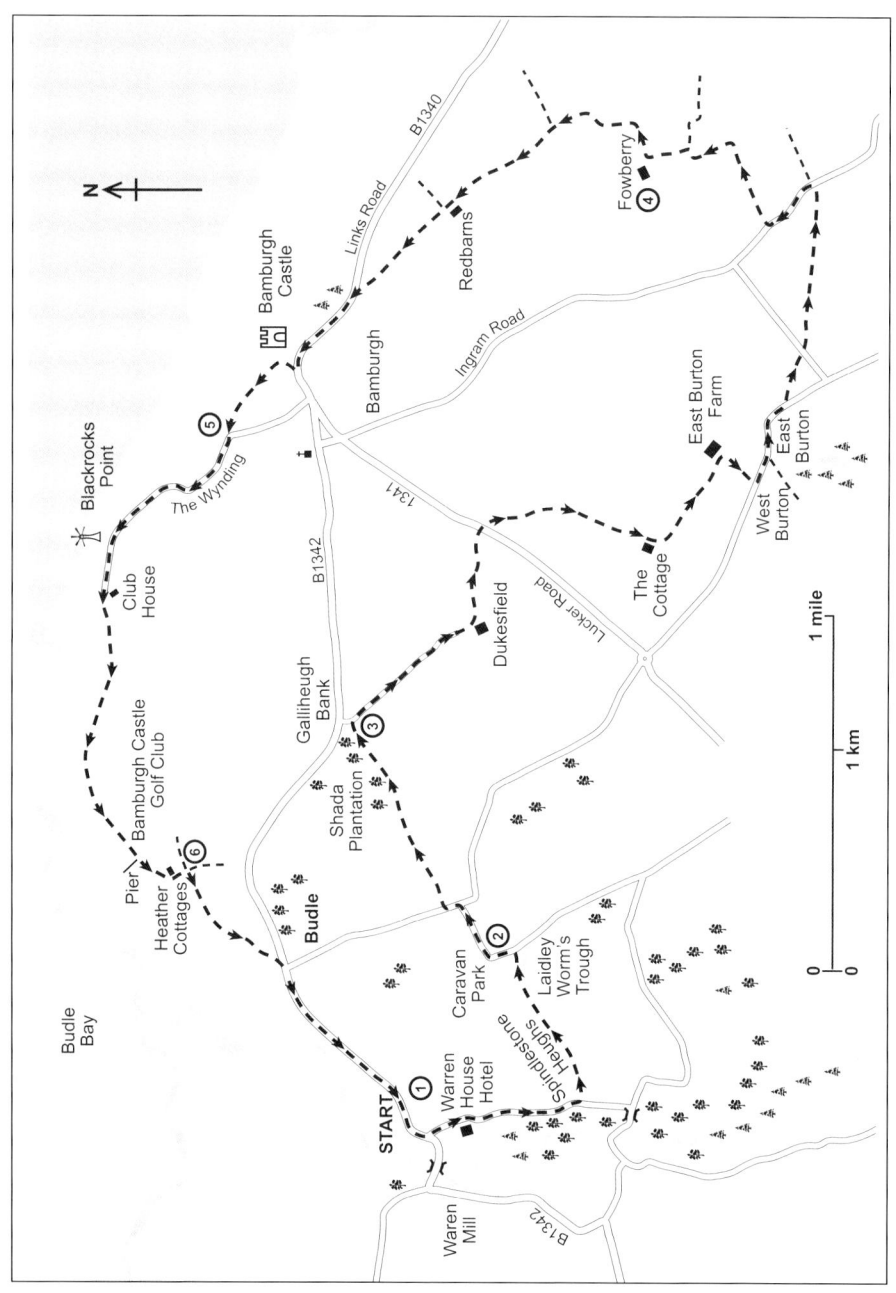

Pass a wicket gate on the left and go on past the Laidley Worm's Trough (marked thus by HM Ordnance Survey!) on the right (usually dry) to go through a gate onto a road.

Lime is made by heating limestone. It was used in mortar, as a stabilizer in renders and floors and to break up heavy clay soils. Permanent lime kilns fall into two broad categories: 'Flare kilns' and 'Draw kilns'. In a flare kiln, a bottom layer of coal was built up and the kiln above filled solely with chalk. The fire was alight for several days, and then the entire kiln was emptied of the lime. In a draw kiln, the chalk was layered with coke and lit. As it burnt through, lime was extracted from the bottom of the kiln and further layers of chalk and coke added to the top

2. Turn left then right at the entrance to Waren Caravan Park. At a T-junction turn left. At a public footpath sign on the right (Bamburgh/Coastal Path) turn right to follow the right edge of a field. Bamburgh Castle is ahead and there are excellent views all round you. Descend to cross a stile and keep ahead on the left of a hedge towards Shada Plantation then down a slope to cross another stile. Head across the shoulder of Galliheugh Hill towards Bamburgh Castle and go through a kissing gate onto a lane.

   NB. You have a choice here. You could turn left up onto the B1342 and turn right to walk (along wide verges and pavement) into Bamburgh, or turn right for the longer route. **The shorter route** follows The Wynding in Bamburgh which is reached by walking down towards the castle and turning left at the end of the village green. The two walk routes rejoin at The Boathouse on The Wynding (see Point 5).

   A heugh is a crag or precipice, a cliff or steep bank. The word is derived from the Old English hōh. The derivation of the Galli prefix of Galliheugh is not so clear though. It may be too fanciful to suggest some connection with gallows. There are a number of other place-names in Northumberland derived from the grim use of locations for hangings. This would be an ideal place!

3. **For the longer route** turn right along the lane to Dukesfield. At Dukesfield cross a stile on the left and follow the fence on your right. Cross a stile into a small field then go diagonally right to cross another. Keep on with a field edge on the right. Cross a stile and a road to follow a hedge enclosed (and possibly muddy and overgrown) bridleway to The Cottage. Pass the

cottage then turn left over a sunken stile to follow a left field edge to East Burton Farm. Keep ahead through a field gate and then another. Turn right along a drive onto a road. Turn left to pass a hamlet of whitewashed cottages and then turn right. Watch out for a signpost to New Shoreston. Go through a wicket gate into a field then diagonally right across a field to cross a stile roughly in the middle of the hedge you are approaching. Cross over a road then over a stile and on ahead in the same diagonal line. At the next stile cross over and keep on the same diagonal to reach two stiles. One will do! Cross onto a road and turn left. At a footpath sign on the right go through a gate and follow a track past an old pillbox and turning left past a wicket gate. Keep on to go through a field gate and onto a metalled lane. Now turn left along this for a few yards to Fowberry.

Fowberry is a family name. The Fowberrys owned an estate near Chatton for over 400 years but they sold out in 1591. It is not clear what the connection will be with this farm though.

4. At the farm turn right along a track. Go through a wide field gate then another and turn sharp left to follow the field edge round to go through a field gate and over a stream. Now follow a stone wall on your right. Go through a wide gate and on ahead through a gap and alongside a new hedge on the right. At the right corner of the field near Redbarns Cottages descend to go through a narrow gap and between fences. Go through a wicket gate, cross a drive, then go through another wicket gate to descend (carefully) into a car parking area. Go up some steps, through a wicket gate, and through a kissing gate into a field. Now follow the fence/wall on the left and, past a field corner, follow a line diagonally right across the field (potentially very muddy) to exit the field via a wicket gate and over a stone step stile onto a road. Turn left along the road beneath the castle passing the main car park. Where the road turns left up to the village cross over the road into the cricket field. Follow a tarmac track right at the base of the huge castle. If you go through a gap in the corner you would join the path down to the beach, but if you continue just turn left in front of the pavilion. Just past it turn right along a signed footpath to join the Wynding at The Boathouse.

The great castle is built on a dolerite outcrop previously home to a British fort until 547. It was captured by the Anglo-Saxon Ida of Bernicia. His grandson Aethelfrith passed it on to his wife Bebba, from whom the early name Bebbanburgh was derived. The Normans built a castle on the site, which forms the core of the present one. William II unsuccessfully besieged it in 1095.

Bamburgh Castle from the children's playground near The Wynding. The great castle is built on a dolerite outcrop

> In 1464 it became the first castle in England to be defeated by artillery. It was owned by the Forster family until 1700 when it was sold to Lord Crew, Bishop of Durham. It was bought in the 19th century by industrialist William Armstrong who restored it. It has been used as a film location since the 1920s, featuring in numerous films such as 'El Cid'. Bamburgh is also famous because of its connection with Grace Darling, the heroine who helped her father to rescue nine people from the wreck of the 'SS Forfarshire' on the Farne Islands in 1838. She is buried in the churchyard of St. Aidan's Church and there is a splendid museum just opposite the church.

5. Now follow the road to the Bamburgh Castle Golf Club. The route continues across the course so read the notice on a white kissing gate which is the start of this section. The route is well marked. It is mostly along the edge of the course and is very often along clear sandy/gravel tracks. It reduces into a good path and leads to a concrete shelter and a signpost with three markers. Follow the footpath marker up the slope on the left to continue along the edge of the golf course and exit through a kissing gate next to a field gate. To the right are static caravans and chalets (Heather Cottages).

6. Turn left along a track and follow the track to reach more chalets where you go through a gate and onto a track. Turn left here then within yards turn right up to a wicket gate to go through and follow a ruined wall on the left. Descend towards a ladder stile (damaged when this was written). Negotiate the stile or go through the field gate next to it. In the field beyond head on a right diagonal to go through a field gate onto the B1342 where you walk back down (carefully) to your car.

(**NB.** At low tide it is possible to walk along the beach on the edge of Budle Bay from near the golf course and continue along the edge of salt marshland to reach the parking area. **NEVER** attempt this unless the tide is well out and not coming in – it moves very quickly.)

Budle Bay is an important bird sanctuary, with huge mud flats that are exposed at low tide. The whole area is part of the Lindisfarne National Nature Reserve and is very popular with birdwatchers. Waren Mill was once an extremely busy port in the 13th century. The harbour has now disappeared beneath the rising silt of the bay. There was a corn-mill here, which is how the hamlet got its name, as early as 1187 and the current building dates back to 1780. After being abandoned for many years it has been redeveloped and turned into luxury apartments.

Budle Bay with the tide out viewed from the golf course. Childe Wynd landed here

WORD SEARCH

e	k	q	q	w	v	f	t	v	b	v	m	q	k	l
n	n	b	x	u	i	e	m	a	z	r	d	y	d	w
o	h	r	g	r	m	t	m	s	o	n	h	i	m	a
t	a	v	m	s	k	b	c	w	m	a	j	b	t	r
s	s	d	p	z	u	s	y	h	c	w	y	p	d	e
e	g	q	h	r	b	e	b	x	c	o	r	k	k	n
l	o	s	g	q	l	z	y	e	w	r	j	s	r	f
d	u	h	o	d	t	e	r	a	g	r	a	m	l	o
n	w	i	i	v	d	n	o	s	b	b	a	f	l	r
i	e	a	d	d	d	e	s	e	d	e	g	u	t	d
p	l	r	e	u	k	i	f	i	c	i	l	h	b	l
s	a	g	y	q	k	j	w	r	b	l	q	d	k	w
c	h	i	l	d	e	w	y	n	d	g	v	f	u	j
d	m	x	t	s	q	z	d	c	d	w	q	f	f	b
p	w	l	s	k	s	q	l	t	e	y	r	t	p	q

Bamburgh
Budlebay
Childewynd
Kiss
Laidleyworm
Margaret
Rowan
Spindlestone
Warenford
Witchcraft

WALK 2
NETHERWITTON AND LONGWITTON

A geordie Dick Whittington? An invisible dragon? The Devil's Elbow? You meet them all on this walk on tracks and along field edges.

THE LONGWITTON DRAGON

Dragons are awesome creatures with a spectacular array of armoury. The usual repertoire includes razor sharp teeth, great talons, fiery breath and the amazing ability to regenerate sections of their bodies as soon as these are sliced off by questing knights. All of those are well encased by impenetrable coats of scales. The famed Longwitton Dragon, though, had another trick up its sleeve (or wing).

Longwitton is a small hamlet in Northumberland. In woods close by there were three wells which were very famous because of the health giving properties of the water. People travelled from far and wide to drink the sweet waters to ease arthritic joints, to ease pains in limbs and to give health to sickly children. The people of Longwitton were proud of their magical wells.

One dreadful day though, a local ploughman went to the wells to quench his thirst after a hard day in the fields. To his horror he found that his route was blocked by an immense serpent which had coiled its great tail around a tree and was noisily lapping water. At the sound of his motion through the trees the monster vanished. It disappeared. Yet the ploughman knew of its presence for he could hear its claws moving on the damp leaves and its great body moving towards him through the dense undergrowth, and could feel its hot breath on his face. In terror he turned and fled through the trees to the safety of the village.

From that day on no pilgrim or villager dared to go to the wells for fear of the dragon. It was a monstrous creature with dense scaly skin, huge wings and a

33

long lizard-like tail. It tore up the ground with its claws. It crashed through the trees causing devastation. At night the villagers had little sleep because of its bellowing. To get their water they now had to walk for miles to the nearest stream. It remained near the wells though, and seemed content to live alone in the woods. Any attempt by the villagers to attack it led to it becoming infuriated, making itself invisible and chasing them away in terror. The wells were unvisited and overgrown.

So things remained for many months. Then one day there came by a questing knight in search of adventure.

The villagers approached their visitor with respect and told him of the disaster which had befallen their small community and for which there seemed to be no solution.

The knight agreed to try and remove the menace and he determined to find an answer to the weapon of invisibility. So he called upon a local witch and she sold him a pot of special ointment. Rubbed on the eyes the ointment countered the invisibility which rendered the beast invulnerable to attack.

So off the visitor rode into the woods of Longwitton, his eyes coated in magic ointment. At the sound of his approach and trusting to its invisibility the dragon reared up and charged towards him. As it tried to strike him with its claws the knight thrust his long sword in its side. The dragon howled with anger and pain because the wound was severe. It backed away towards the wells, and then seemed prepared to attack again. In fact no matter how dreadful the wounds which the knight inflicted the dragon seemed to recover its strength and attack again. No sooner were wounds made than they healed over. So for hours the knight and the dragon fought each other. The clumsy dragon could not match the nimbleness of the man, but the knight became exhausted from the conflict and was forced, at last, to withdraw to his horse and return to the village.

The next day the knight resolved to return and resume the conflict and the style of the previous day was repeated. No matter how many blows he delivered the dragon seemed always able to return to fight him with the same strength. So he was forced to retire yet again then attempt again on the third day.

On the third occasion though the knight determined to observe more carefully the behavior of the dragon to see if it was possible to see the source of its

Longwitton Dragon

strength. He realized that no matter how hard he fought the beast it would not be moved away from the wells, and looking more closely he saw that its tail was always dipped in the magic waters. That was the origin of the remarkable ability of the dragon to reinvigorate itself.

This time the knight adopted a different course of action. Dismounting from his horse he wound his way round the dragon, darting in and out as quickly as possible to thrust his sword into its great carcase to madden it and make it leap at him and chase him. Then the knight retreated as if weakened and wounded so as to lure the beast on towards him – and away from the magical wells. So as it came closer to him he suddenly leapt upon his faithful horse and rode round behind the dragon, between it and the wells. When this had been accomplished the dragon saw how it had been tricked and bellowed like a mad bull as it tried to return to the magical waters. Now the knight knew that he was the master. He dealt the dragon blow by blow, driving it away further and further from the wells. Blood dripped from its flanks, its strength dwindled and soon it fell heavily on its side and died.

The next day the villagers of Longwitton entered the woods and buried the dead body of their old enemy. They tidied the wells and sent out news that the dragon was no more and the way to the wells was opened. There was great rejoicing throughout the area.

The knight, his work done, rode on in search of new adventures.

NOTES

There is a tiny hamlet called Longwitton near Morpeth in Northumberland. There are the remains of a medieval village and medieval field patterns just to the west of this. At various times Longwitton Hall belonged to the Swinburnes, the Trevelyans, the Fenwicks and the Percevals. There is a haugh called the Dragon's Den near Hartburn. There were once three mineral springs called the Holy Wells near Hartburn as well and they appear on the Ordnance Survey map as such. On the other hand some versions of the story do say that the wells were in the grounds of Longwitton Hall – and indeed there are wells there. So as with most dragon tales the features match the narrative !

One of the wells at Longwitton Hall. However it is claimed that the wells were nearer Hartburn

Of course in nearly all dragon stories the presence of water in some form is significant. There are also numerous myths and legends where magical waters or other features are guarded by guardians – although not normally to exclude worshippers or users in quite the selfish way of the Longwitton Dragon.The

Holy Wells will have been 'treacle wells'! 'Treacle' meant 'a medicine', derived from the Greek 'theriacal' meaning medicinal (Gk *theriake* = a *curative* or *antidote*), so the various healing wells around Britain were called 'treacle wells'.

According to some accounts the travelling Clint Eastwood-style knight was none other than the great professional dragon (and giant) killer Sir Guy of Warwick who lived, supposedly, in the reign of King Athelstan and undertook adventures all over Europe to prove himself to his lady-love Felice. Most of these knights appear from nowhere – just passing through or returning from 'foreign wars'. It enhances the effect in communities which would be living in isolation.

There is no clear evidence as to the date of the origin of the story. Certainly it appears in *The Reliques of Ancient English Poetry* (sometimes known as *Reliques of Ancient Poetry* or simply *Percy's Reliques*) a collection of ballads and popular songs collected by Bishop Thomas Percy and published in 1765.

THE WALK

What you need to know	
Distance	6.5 miles or 6 miles
Time	3.5 hours or 3 hours
Map	Ordnance Survey Explorer 325 Morpeth and Blyth
Starting point	St. Giles Church, Netherwitton. There is a small parking area near the church. Otherwise roadside parking. Grid Reference NZ100902
Terrain	Mostly riverside and woodland paths, tracks and field edges. There are no steep gradients but it can be very muddy in some sections. Mostly old farmland. There are a couple of sections of road walking. Please note that in the final section there is a small ford to cross. While usually dry it could be water-covered in periods of heavy rainfall
How to get there	Netherwitton is about seven and a half miles north west of Morpeth via the A192. Postcode for SatNav: NE61 4NU (Netherwitton Mill)

| Refreshments | None at Netherwitton. The nearest would be the Dyke Neuk *en route* to Morpeth |

1. Walk back down the lane from St. Giles Church passing Netherwitton Mill. Turn right across the picturesque bridge over the Font. Turn left along a road. Pass a footpath sign on the left and keep on. Turn off on a bridleway on the left (signed Needlesshallmoor!) passing through a pair of wide gates. Now follow the woodland track. Ignore side tracks and keep on to descend a slope on a (muddy) path by a stream. At a wicket gate go through then turn right to go through another. Follow a grassy track on ahead with a fence over on the left to reach a kissing gate next to a wide gate. Go through this to join a road at Thornton Moor.

   Netherwitton was bought by a Dick Whittington-type Mayor of Newcastle, Roger Thornton, in 1405, who built or rebuilt the church. Thornton is claimed to have been born there but there are alternative views

St. Giles Church at Netherwitton

as to his origins. Thornton was a speculator in lead mines, and he was certainly working some in Weardale under lease from the Bishop of Durham in 1401. He was remembered for his liberality to Newcastle of which he was mayor on nine occasions as well as representing it in parliament. Thornton died in 1430. His monumental brass is now in Newcastle Cathedral and is said to be the largest brass in the country. St. Giles's Church was consecrated in the 15th Century. A life sized effigy, probably of Agnes Thornton, is worth seeing. Netherwitton Mill was a cotton mill built in 1794 which has been restored and converted into apartments.

Effigy of Agnes Thornton. Her husband Roger was the Dick Whittington of Tyneside

2. Turn right along this quiet road but stay alert for traffic. Where the road bends right turn left up an (unsigned) track to Wittonstone Farm. Go through a wide gate into the farmyard and keep left of the buildings to go through double field gates and past the farmhouse. Stay with the track past barns. Then at a fence corner turn left on the track and keep ahead through more wide field gates towards a small copse. There turn right along a bridleway then go left through a gap in the field boundary and

Netherwitton Mill was a cotton mill built in 1794 which has been restored and converted into apartments

turn right to follow the field edge. In the corner of the field go through a gap and down a short track (muddy) towards a stream. Cross a footbridge

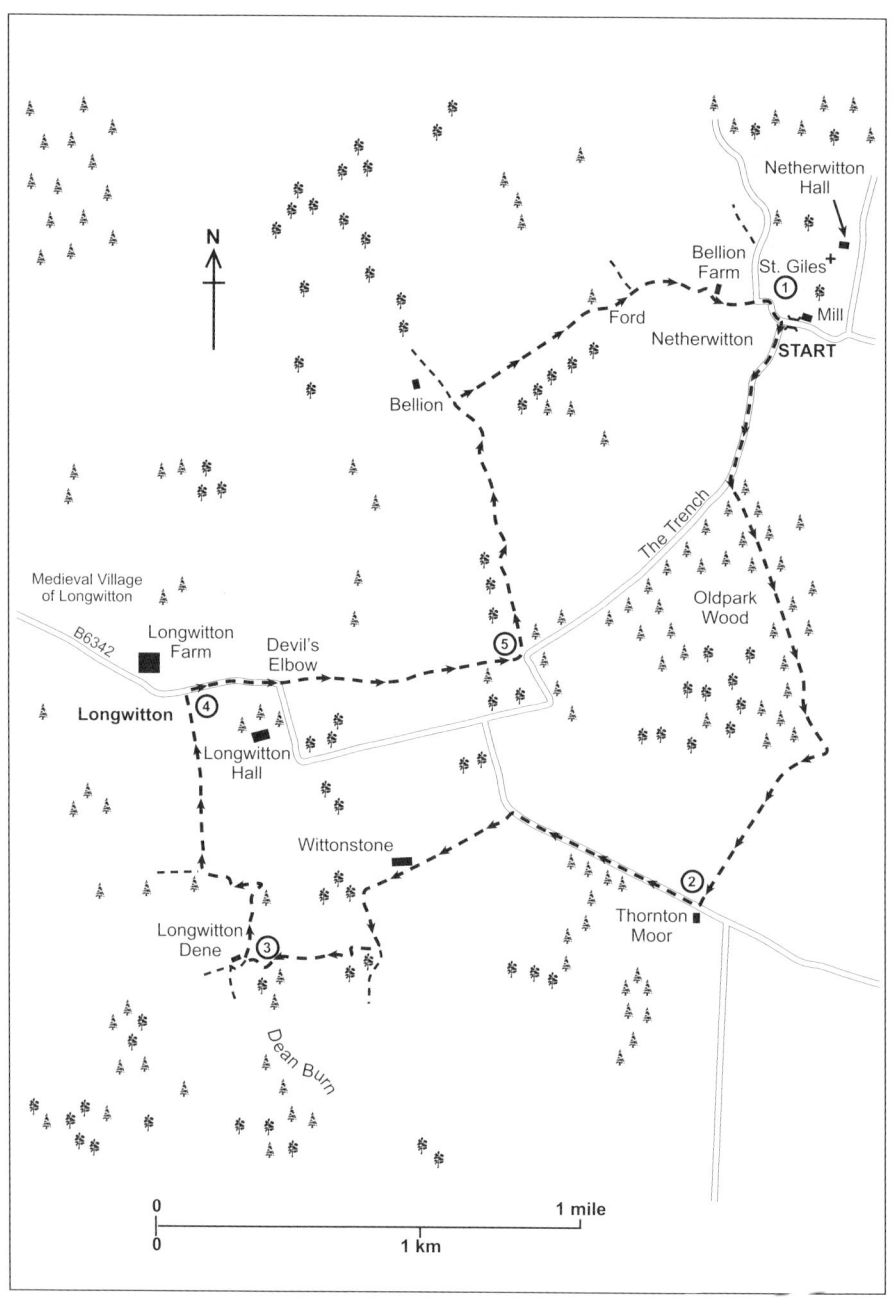

next to a noisy lake dam overflow. Go up the track opposite (even muddier) to reach a three way finger post.

3. Turn right here on a track to Longwitton/Southwitton. Cross another ford/footbridge then at a signed footpath on the left go off the track to cross an awkward stile. Now follow the left edge of the field ahead until you reach a gap in the corner. Go through the gap and then turn right to follow the field edge again, ie. on the left side of the hedge. Keep on the path up a very gradual slope and on through a gap in the field corner. Exit via difficult double field gates onto the road at Longwitton.

The origin of the names Longwitton, Wittonstone and Netherwitton will have been based on a combination of the Old English (OE) words widu = wood *and* tun = settlement *giving* widutun *which eventually shortens over time to* witun *(spelt thus in 1236). So* Netherwitton *will have been the* lower wood settlement. *Traces of a medieval village can be seen at Long Witton. There are earthwork banks and platforms where houses used to stand, together with the outlines of gardens or yards.*

4. Turn right along the road towards the so-called Devil's Elbow. Past a cottage, and just before the sharp right-turn sign, turn off the road to follow a footpath sign to 'Spencer's Plantation' on a woodland path which takes you through to exit into a field where you turn right to follow the field edge, passing a wide gap on the right. At the field corner do not cross the inviting stile on the right but just keep on along an enclosed track between field boundaries. Keep on past a redundant stile and follow the path through the woodland edge. Exit onto a quiet road known as The Trench and less than a mile from Netherwitton.

5. Where you exit on to the road at a sharp bend there is a wide double field gate on the left and a sign Devil's Elbow/Keyhirst Hill. Go through the gate and follow a good track ahead with trees to the right. Keep down to a wooden hurdle (waymarked) on the edge of a wood. Go through this and enter the wood. Follow an overgrown path through the woodland edge. It is 'trippy', and beware of fallen trees. Take care with your eyes. Exit via a wooden hurdle on the right. A couple of yards beyond this turn left on a track to cross the Whelpsley Burn and go up to a wide metal field gate. Go through this then follow a grassy path near the right field edge. Aim for the right field corner just beyond, and below a few mature trees. Go through a wicket gate and on a couple of yards to turn left and cross a

little burn and go up into a field. Follow the left edge on up to reach a clear wide track to Bellion. Turn right along this and step out. On the left side is a fence, ditch and trees. Keep on along this bridleway. Go through one wide field gate and then on and through another. You reach a ford. This is usually dry and easy but could be covered if there has been a lot of rain recently. Keep on to skirt to the right of the Bellion Farm, between barns and then past houses on the left and a graveyard on the right. At Netherwitton turn right to cross a road bridge then turn left past the war memorial and across the hump backed road bridge where you turn left up to St. Giles church.

Netherwitton Hall is a Grade I listed building built in about 1685 to a design by architect Robert Trollope. There are remnants of ancient fortifications embodied in it though. During the Civil War, Cromwell quartered a large force in the grounds, and later awarded a sum of £95-5s-6d, as

Longwitton Hall from the south

42

compensation for the damage done by his troops. After Culloden in 1746 Lord Lovat, a Jacobite leader was concealed in a 'Priest's Hole' in an upper room of the Hall. The Devil's Causeway passes the village less than a mile to the east. The causeway is a Roman road which starts at Port Gate on Hadrian's Wall, north of Corbridge, and extends 55 miles northwards across Northumberland to the mouth of the River Tweed at Berwick-upon-Tweed.

CROSSWORD

Across
1. The people who live in a village
3. The same as enormous but frightening as well
6. The unusual feature of this dragon
8. A farm worker
9. The dragon tried to stay close to these
10. The name of the county

Down
2. The name of the village threatened by the dragon
4. A word for the tangled vegetation on the woodland floor
5. What the witch gave to the knight
7. A word which means 'could not be killed'

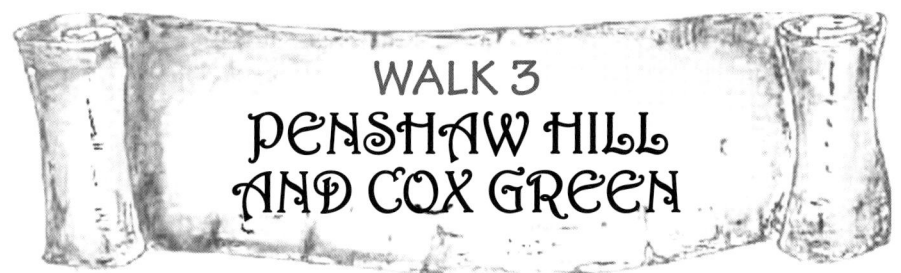

WALK 3
PENSHAW HILL AND COX GREEN

This is the classic British dragon tale and is dominated throughout by the famous Penshaw Monument in a walk following field edges and tracks and the 'Keelmen's Way' along the riverside.

THE LAMBTON WORM

Young John Lambton, the heir to Lambton Castle and the family estate, was a rebellious boy who showed little regard for the dignity and responsibilities of his future role. Instead he preferred to waste away his time in the company of the other rowdy boys of the neighbourhood. He scorned his tutors and defied the wishes of his old father. He delighted in breaking every rule laid down for his guidance. Above all on Sundays he would miss church and go off in his old clothes to fish. Indeed much of the time he could be seen fishing in the River Wear.

One Sunday he was idly casting his line into the river. There he sat, when he should have set an example by being in church with his father, while local folk passed him by and complained to each other about the behavior of their future Lord. He sat there for many hours without even seeing a fish. Again and again he cast his line. Again and again it came up empty. Again and again he cursed loudly the river, the day and his ill luck.

Then at last he felt as if he had a catch. He drew in his line and his rod bent. Indeed he thought he had caught a fine salmon so much did it struggle. However when he had finally landed the catch it was no more than an evil-looking creature, half newt and half eel, which wriggled and wrapped itself around his line.

Lambton Worm

Disgusted at the sight of the beast, and furious at his bad fortune, Lambton tore the worm from his hook and hurled it down a well before storming off back to the castle. He gave no more thought to it for many years.

Young Lambton went off to be a squire in another noble household and there he learnt the skills and duties of a knight. When he reached manhood he took the cross and went off to fight in the Crusades.

Meanwhile back at home things did not go so well. For some years the worm lived unheeded in the well, and grew and grew until it was monstrous. Finally it was able to climb from the well and slither over the edge and make its way to a great ledge of rock jutting from the middle of the river where it was able to lie and bask. From there it took itself on to a hill not far from the castle where it was able to coil itself around three times, so long was it by now.

From these resting places the Lambton Worm began to go on marauding expeditions into the surrounding countryside in search of food. It devoured sheep and lambs, and it sucked the cows dry. When the flocks and herds were moved into the safety of folds and byres it rampaged across the cornfields and devastated the crops.

The old Lord of Lambton was, by now, a very old man. He was driven to his wit's end by the damage caused to his estate and his people by the beast. So notorious had it become that knights journeyed to the Lambton estate from areas far afield to seek to gain a reputation and fortune and glory by killing the monster. However most came to grief because whenever part of its scaly body was cut off it would rejoin the whole at once. No matter into how many parts it was severed it assembled itself again and continued to fight with fiery breath and enormous claws. Even the very best of the knights had not the ability to put an end to it. So for seven long awful years it remained in possession of its hill and enjoyed untrammeled access to the lands along the river sides.

Then one day the once ne'er-do-well son of Lambton returned from his foreign wars. By now he was no longer a rough and shabby youth but was a man of great stature and courage with many years of experience in fighting some of the most able enemies. When he heard of the trouble inflicted upon his father and the Lambton estate he swore that he would end it – as he had been the cause of it so many years before on that fine summer day.

However before he went to encounter the creature he set out to find an answer to the magical powers it possessed. He turned, in fact, to a wise old witch who lived near-by. Her advice was sound. She told him to confront the worm on its favourite rock in the middle of the Wear and to let it attack him there. He was to have made for himself a suit of armour which was studded with cleverly fashioned blades so that as the beast attempted to crush him in its coils it would cut itself to pieces which would then wash away down the river.

Thankful for this help the young knight asked what the price would be for the help of the witch. Her answer was thus:

"You must repay me by observing only one condition. When you have killed the worm and return home you must kill the first living thing you meet. If you fail to do so, the lords of Lambton for nine generations will never die peacefully in their beds."

The young knight hurried home to tell his father the good news that he knew at last how to master the beast. Yet he was also possessed of some cunning and had a plan to deal with the condition laid down by the witch. He said to his father that when the deed was done, and when the worm was dead, he would blow a bugle to alert him. Then his father was to let loose one of his old hounds. It would run to greet the young lord, and be the first living thing he met.

So with the preparations made, and with the suit of bladed armour made by the local blacksmith, young Lambton set off to face the worm at its lair. He had little time to wait for it to return. No sooner did it see him than it bellowed with rage and attempted to seize him. With one blow he sliced away a section of its thrashing tail. Then he saw how wise had been the advice of the witch because the bloody slice of tail was carried away by the swift waters of the ebbing waters of the Wear.

The great beast then coiled itself about Lambton's body but the tighter it grasped him the deeper the blades cut into it and the more furious it became. He managed to free his arm and cut off more of its body which, piece by piece, floated off down the river. At last the triumphant knight stood victorious on the rock.

Then, according to plan, he made his way back towards the castle and his father. He blew his bugle to signal his victory and trigger the release of the hound. To his horror though, he saw that his father had, in his joy, forgotten to let the hound go ahead of him and had rushed to embrace his son. The son could not fulfil his promise to the witch since his own father was the first living creature he met. Hoping to avert the curse he thrust his sword into the hound loping along by his father in the hope that the price would be still paid.

It was in vain though. Although there was great rejoicing throughout the land which had been freed from the menace the curse of the witch was not lifted. From that day not one of the Lords of Lambton died in bed for nine generations.

NOTES

The Lambton Worm is, arguably, the most famous of the dragon stories of the British Isles. It was the basis of *The Lair of the White Worm* (also known as *The Garden of Evil*) a horror novel by Bram Stoker published in 1911, upon which was based a (totally forgettable) film by Ken Russell in 1988. For children the best account is a delightful illustrated version by Joan Henderson. The legend may actually date from the 14th century but it is especially memorable because of the famous music hall song written in 1867 by C. M. Leumane, which passed into oral tradition and is heard at its most effective when sung in a regional accent. Indeed it is virtually the 'national anthem' of County Durham regularly sung enthusiastically at events.

Various landmarks are associated with the story. There is a Worm Hill at Biddick. There was once a significant rock in the middle of the channel which was blasted away by the River Wear Commissioners in the 19th century. Knowledgeable locals will point sagely at the track marks around the prominent Penshaw Hill and tell gullible visitors that they are the marks of the coils of the Lambton Worm.

The Lambton family is an ancient line which may predate the Norman Conquest. They became very wealthy from the late 18th century on the basis of the coal found on their lands. Many of the Lambtons did die violent deaths, but then they would because they were frequently serving as soldiers. Two of them died in the Royalist cause in the English Civil Wars. The last of the nine generations, Henry Lambton, died in his carriage of a heart attack while crossing Lambton Bridge on 26th June, 1761. Hopeful children still fish along the banks.

There are several versions of the story, which has thus, like the beast, "growed an awful size". Of course it is patently obvious that the story is also, or was

The Biddick Inn with Worm Hill to the left. The crocodile sculpture is probably near the origin of dragon stories

Penshaw Monument in the late 19th Century. This view is taken from a point near the end of your walk

made, a moralistic one, because Lambton brought this all upon his House because he did not go to church when he should have done. The curious story about the old hound and the father is in the same category as that of the death of Aegeus the father of Theseus, who also killed a monster by a combination of guile and courage, who is misled by an agreed signal not being implemented.

It is a great story though!

THE WALK

What you need to know	
Distance	A figure-of-eight walk. 6 miles for the full circular walk or 5 miles if you get too comfortable at the Oddfellows Arms
Time	3.5 hours or 3 hours
Map	Ordnance Survey Explorer 308 Durham and Sunderland
Starting point	The lay-by on the south side of Penshaw Hill. Alternatively for a shorter version park at the car park near the Oddfellows Arms. Grid Reference NZ335541 for the lay-by and Grid Reference NZ327552 for the Oddfellows Arms
Terrain	There are a couple of short steep inclines. Beware of the unfenced steep riverside edge in places. In some riverside stretches there is giant hogweed – but usually well out of reach
How to get there	The lay-by is just off the A182 (Chester Road) between Penshaw and Sunderland. Postcode for SatNav: DH4 7NJ (The Penshaw Nursery and Tea Room) or SR4 9JS (the Oddfellows Arms)
Refreshments	The Penshaw Nursery and Tea Room, the Oddfellows Arms and the Biddick Inn are on the route. The Grey Horse at Penshaw is not far off the route either

1. From the lay-by go through a kissing gate by an information board and up to the monument. Pass to the right of it and keep on over the hill crest to follow a wide grassy track to reach a stile at the edge of the Penshaw Wood. Cross this and follow the path along the woodland edge. Cross/pass a stile and keep on. Cross another stile to follow a fence on the right above a steeply sloping field and the remnants of quarrying. Exit across a stile onto a sharp right turn on a minor road. Turn right and follow the road towards Offerton.

Penshaw Monument was erected in 1844 to commemorate 'Radical Jack' John Lambton, the First Earl of Durham, the first Governor of Canada, author of the influential Durham Report supporting colonial self government and one of the leaders in the passing of the 1832 Parliamentary Reform Act. Designed by John and Benjamin Green it was opened in the presence of a crowd of some 10,000 people. The site and monument are in

Penshaw Monument was erected in 1844 to commemorate 'Radical Jack' John Lambton, the First Earl of Durham

the good care of the National Trust who occasionally open the stairway to the walkway around the top for members of the public.

2. At a right bend keep ahead through Offerton past Offerton Hall Farm on the right ('River Wear ¾'). Turn left and double back down a slope between houses and turn right to go down an old enclosed tarmac lane. At Railway Crossing Cottage and cross-tracks keep on ahead down the Offerton 'Lonnen' and follow the pleasant hedged track down to the Wear riverside. At the riverside turn left across a stile along the unfenced path to Cox Green. In places the undulating path rises high above the river. Eventually descend a long dog-legged flight of steps and cross a little footbridge to reach the bottom of Copperas Gill. Keep on along the riverside path. Cross another small footbridge and go through a final kissing gate to arrive back at Cox Green – and the Oddfellows Arms. At this point you have a choice. You can continue on the longer version or follow a shorter route – in which case you would resume the walk directions at 5 and skip the riverside stretch to the Biddick Inn and back.

Railway Crossing Cottage viewed from the Offerton Lonnin. It stands on the line of the old Sunderland Railway track

Although now largely forgotten, the copperas industry was once a highly significant one. Copperas, or iron vitriol, is a ferrous sulphate. It was made from iron pyrites stone which was a waste product of coal-mining. Typically beds of pyrites were laid out with a trough at the bottom to collect the liquor resulting from rainfall. Copperas was used to make black and red dyes. Other possible uses included production of sulphuric acid, or oil of vitriol, dye fixative, ink and gunpowder manufacture. Oddfellows Lodges dating back to the 18th century were set up to protect and care for their members at a time when there was no welfare state. This inn will have been a meeting place for the society which will have covered local keelmen and miners.

3. From the Oddfellows Arms keep on along the riverside past Alice's Well Villas, the Cox Green footbridge and then Alice's Well (1895). Go through a metal kissing gate and keep on to pass underneath the Victoria Viaduct.

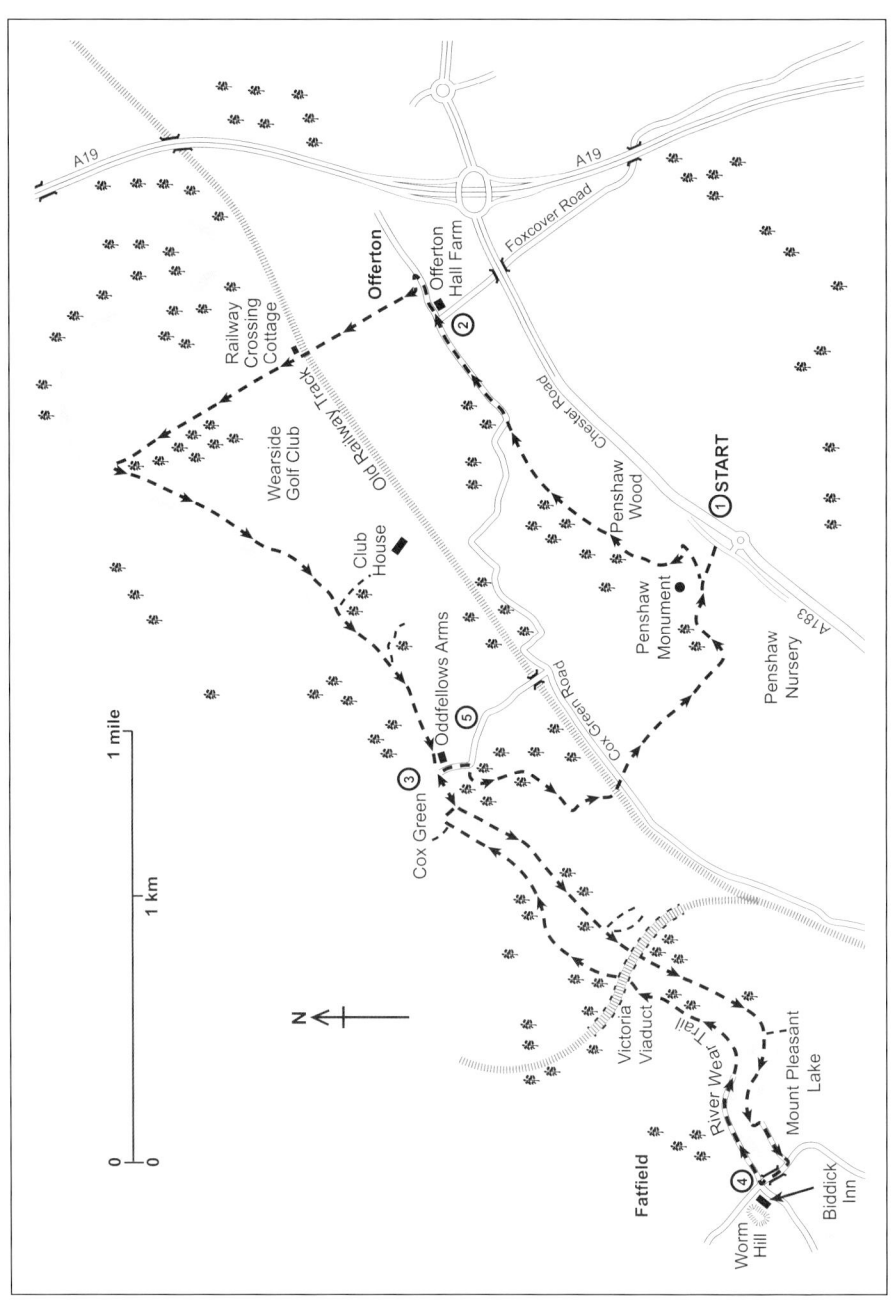

Continue on along the track which is fenced in places for good reason. Go through another metal gate and pass the Mount Pleasant Lake. Keep right at a path fork and ahead past terraced cottages to arrive at the Biddick Bridge. Cross the bridge. The welcoming Biddick Inn is to the left on Bonemill Lane.

Behind the Biddick Inn is Worm Hill. According to some accounts it was around this that the Lambton Worm coiled itself between excursions to 'swally bairns' and so forth. The River Bar (formerly the 'The Inn Between') is an old Cooperative Building built in 1909 standing between the Biddick Inn and the General Havelock Inn. The Victoria Viaduct is modelled on a Roman aqueduct at Alcantara in Spain and was built to carry the Durham junction of the North Eastern Railway. It was opened on the day of the coronation of Queen Victoria in 1838. It is no longer in use. On the south side at its base are the steps and landing which were used by a ferry connecting Penshaw and North Biddick Colliery. The Low Lambton Staithes stood close by.

Biddick Bridge

4. Turn right along the lane on the north side of the river past a row of riverside terraced houses (South View) and then Biddick Pumping Station – formerly the site of the famous Girdle Cake Cottage. Keep on along the lane ignoring paths to the left. Pass under the Victoria Viaduct again then at Victoria Bridge House follow a narrower track and, via a metal gate, a fenced riverside path. Go between black metal barriers and fork turn right to go through a copse, then across an open grassy area to the Cox Green bridge which you cross.

The Cox Green footbridge was opened in 1958. Until then the river was crossed by means of a rowing ferry. On the opposite bank was Low Barmston which was once overshadowed by the waste heaps of a huge chemical works. There was once a thriving little community there with a chapel, mission hall and two public houses. This was all swept away with the development of the new town of Washington and the James Steel Park. The white walled and red tiled Girdle Cake Cottage catered until the 1930s for day-trippers coming up the river and was renowned for its ham and egg teas. However it was also reputed as being the residence of James Drummond, the Earl of Perth, who supposedly took refuge here after the Battle of Culloden. There is a gravestone in the churchyard of Penshaw Church where the self-styled Third Earl of Perth was buried. Descendants still exist and claim the title.

5. From the Oddfellows Arms go up the road (still signed for Cox Green Station) past the drive to Church House. Cross a stile on the right then follow a good path alongside then across a dene. Go past a stile and beyond a large barn go through a wicket gate in a field corner (signed) and follow the left field edge to cross a (difficult) stile onto a farm drive then onto an old railway track. Cross the track, and the minor road, and then cross a stile next to a wide gate and keep on up the left field edge. Where the track forks the right of way is the left fork across a stile, along a right field edge and then across a second stile onto a track (but if you follow the other fork it brings you to the same spot more easily!). Turn left along the hedge-enclosed track and keep on round past a wide gate and past steps on the left (to the monument) and on between a hedge and wire fence. At a wide metal gate go through a kissing gate and keep on ahead to descend steps to the field and your start.

The name of Penshaw is an amalgam of the Celtic pen = hill *and Saxon* shaw = wood *ie. a* wooded hill.

ANAGRAMS

These words have been mixed up.

Can you unscramble

kchbtmasli	lambton
rcdsucas	blacksmith
kibdicd	generation
ienenrotag	sword
earw	wear
srdow	penshaw
ecusr	hound
ohdnu	curse
anphwse	crusades
tobmlan	biddick

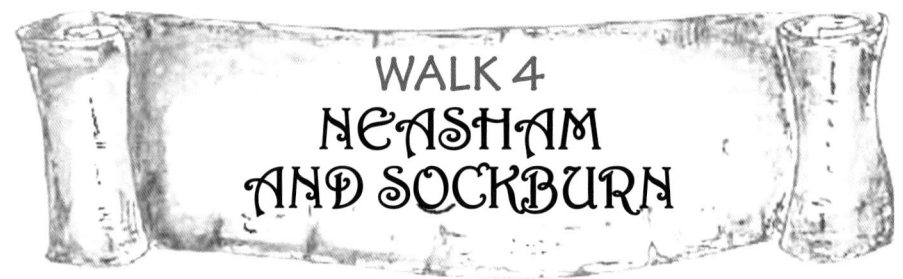

WALK 4
NEASHAM AND SOCKBURN

This story has many of the standard ingredients – but adds for flavouring the Bishop of Durham, William Wordsworth and a very real sword wielded by the, supposed, dragon killer. A quiet lane and field-walking make up much of the route.

THE SOCKBURN WORM

The people living along the banks of the Tees once lived in great terror of an awful dragon. A monstrous and evil beast it used its huge crashing jaws and poisonous breath to great effect. It flew easily through the air attacking the poor people who dwelt along the Tees. Death, devastation and famine haunted the land and resulted in great sadness and despair.

No-one knew at all where the creature had come from. However all knew where it lived. It made a lair near a well beside the tree-lined banks of the Tees in a loop in the river between Yarm and Darlington. There it lurked. In the daytime it sheltered from the rays of the sun. Then when it was hungry it ventured forth on its murderous mission.

The local inhabitants resorted to trying to fill the appetite of the beast with the milk from their cows. They built a huge trough and filled it daily with fresh milk from their cattle. But this was not enough to assuage the needs of the dragon. And when it had drunk the milk and rested its great body it would return to attack and destroy as before.

Now the Lord of the Manor of Sockburn was a knight called Sir John Conyers. To challenge such a beast was an immense danger but eventually he decided that only he could save his land and people. So he dressed himself in his full armour and went to the chapel of All Saints to ask for the blessing of God upon his venture. In the dark silence of the old chapel he prayed for the deliverance of the lands of the Tees from this devil. Sir John spent the whole night in vigil before the altar. Then he returned to his hall and took up his great sword – the Conyers Falchion. The Falchion was a great, single-edged sword, a yard in length. It had been blooded may times in battle so it felt very easy and familiar in his hand.

At the first light of the day Sir John went forth to the fields of Sockburn with his great hound. At the well he waited for the return of the dragon. Then, as the sun rose and the heat grew the dragon returned – full of the flesh of the sheep and the cattle of the poor peasants. It sought out its lair to lie and rest but what it found was the light of the sun on the edge of Sir John's great sword.

The monster roared its great noise and blew across the knight its poisoned breath. But he stood fearlessly, and, with the help of his god, withstood the poison. Then the real battle began as the huge creature endeavoured to grip the knight in its coils and to destroy him with its huge teeth and slashing claws. However the armour of the knight was strong and withstood the test well. In fact the knight was caught within the huge coils and it took all of his remaining strength to cut and thrust with his Falchion. Finally though, he managed to bring his sword down with one last swing and he felt it cut through the skin and flesh of the dragon, separating its head from its leathery neck and spouting dark blood into the silvery waters of the Tees. So the task was done. Sir John knelt and prayed to thank God for his help and for the strength of his armour and his sword.

Then the people came and rejoiced at their freeing from the beast which had tormented them for so long. The danced and they feasted. However before they ate and drank Sir John had them take the huge body and bury it in a great pit. Then they took a great grey slab of limestone and laid it over the top of the grave.

The King of the land heard of this great victory and he rewarded the lords of Sockburn by giving the manor forever to them and to their descendants. And to mark the deed forever he ordered that the Falchion, the weapon which had been so true in the hand of the knight, should be presented symbolically to each new Prince Bishop of Durham as he crossed the Tees at Sockburn to enter Durham.

NOTES

The Conyers Falchion is one of the great treasures of Durham Cathedral. In recent times the old tradition of presenting it to incoming bishops of Durham has been revived. It was held for centuries at Sockburn Hall, the ancestral hall of the Conyers family. Now it is held in the Treasury of the Cathedral to be admired by visitors. According to different versions of the story the exchange should take place at Sockburn or Neasham Fords or at Croft. In 1661 there is a reference to the 'usual ceremony' when Bishop John Cosin crossed the Tees. This was associated with a recitation of the nature of the deed for which the sword had been used. In fact the ceremony may date from 1386.

There is a dent on the curve of the blade – perhaps a result of the last desperate thrust! It is beautifully made and highly decorated with engravings of grotesque creatures on the guard. It has been suggested that the sword was produced and thus engraved to celebrate the deed rather than being the weapon with which the deed was performed. It has been dated at c.1260-1270 but it might be older. The Blacketts who inherited the Falchion attached a label to it with the date 1063 on it as the date when the dragon was killed. However that would not be possible if the sword was produced 200 years later – unless it was a copy of an original.

The Conyers family ended in 1810 when the last descendant died destitute. By then their lands had been taken over by the great Blackett family from Newcastle. The Conyers family had been one of the greatest in the North. It is claimed that the effigy of a knight in the ruins of the chapel close to the hall is that of Sir John himself. If you are wondering who exchanges the sword with incoming bishops nowadays it is the Mayor of Darlington.

The Chapel of All Saints is now very ruinous. It stands only twenty yards from the Tees. It contains not only the effigy but also a collection of bits of Viking sculptures with both Norse and Christian imagery. There is also a hogback Viking gravestone. Intriguingly it is embellished with an image of the battle between Tyr the Norse god and the giant wolf Fenyr. The chapel was once used for the crowning of Higbald in 781 as Bishop of Lindisfarne and also for Eanbald as Archbishop of York in 796. So Sockburn was a significant place. Sadly the chapel was only reduced to such a ruined state in recent times because the Blacketts wanted a romantic gothic ruin to gaze upon from their new Victorian hall. The chapel and the hall are now in private hands and the land around the former is badly overgrown.

Sockburn was also the romantic setting for the meeting of William Wordsworth with his future wife Mary Hutchinson. In fact some people have claimed that *The Daffodils* is more properly associated with the banks of the Tees – but the need to encourage tourism is a great driving force. His friend Coleridge – already married – also fell in love with her sister Sara and penned a (poor) poem about Love. The tale is also said by many to be the inspiration for Lewis Carroll's poem *Jabberwocky* which he wrote while in Croft-on-Tees and Whitburn.

The Greystone also survives. It stands on private ground and is hidden by crops in the summer. The local farmer is constantly pestered by visitors who want to see the stone and, good naturedly, constantly agrees to let them. The great slab is cracked – the result of a farmer trying to move it once. He might have been curious, and wanting to see what remained of the dragon. Certainly the field is a very fertile one and so the corpse of a huge dragon might have helped in that respect. Greystones appear elsewhere in legends. In Beowulf the hero fights the dragon at the 'harne stan' and dies there. In fact Tolkien has a greystone at the entrance to Smaug's treasure.

As far as the well and the foul fumes breathed by the dragon are concerned it has been suggested that this aspect is related to the very real prevalence of sulphur wells in this area. Indeed Dinsdale Spa nearby at Middleton-One-Row became famous as a resort where the curative sulphur waters could be taken. So perhaps the poisonous breath of the dragon was no more than the smell of sulphur ?

The Grey Stone at Sockburn. It is claimed that the remains of the Sockburn Worm are buried beneath this

Perhaps because so many physical, tangible features of the story of the Sockburn Worm survive it has given rise to a tremendous range of proposed explanations.

THE WALK

What you need to know	
Distance	8 miles
Time	4.5 hours
Map	Ordnance Survey Explorer 304 Darlington and Richmond
Starting point	The Fox and Hounds in Neasham. Roadside parking in the village. Grid Reference NZ324101
Terrain	Mostly tracks and field paths. There is road walking at the start of the walk and again in the middle but the roads concerned are quiet. No steep gradients but some sections can be very muddy
How to get there	Neasham is 6 miles south east of Darlington. It is connected by minor roads to the A66 (T) and A67. Postcode for SatNav: DL21QP (The Fox and Hounds)

| Refreshments | The Fox and Hounds in Neasham which is your starting and end point |

1. Go up the left side of the Fox and Hounds on a signed public footpath through the inn backyard. Go up steps onto the flood defence barrier and turn left to walk along the top. Cross a stile then continue between fences to exit via a stile onto Sockburn Lane. Turn right along this quiet lane passing The Lodge, a couple of cottages then Rose Cottage. Ignore the sign on the left for the Teesdale Way (you will return that way). Keep on past piles of timber and Liberty Lodge (a gable end plaque reads 'Liberty Lodge 1872'). Stay with the hedge-lined lane to reach High Sockburn where a sign says 'Private Property: Keep Out' (Visits to Sockburn Hall and Sockburn Church can be arranged occasionally with the owners). Turn left through a wicket gate signed 'Teesdale Way' and follow the clear bridleway track down the right side of a hedge. It bends right to Blackett's Bridge.

Sockburn Hall. Sockburn was the romantic setting for the meeting of William Wordsworth with his future wife Mary

Sockburn derives its name from the Old English burg = fortified settlement *of Socca rather than the more obvious* burn *which is not a name used for streams in this area. Neasham must have had a cattle farm because the Old English* neat = cattle *and* ham = settlement. *Liberty Lodge is an intriguing name. The year 1872 is when the right to vote in secret was introduced by law – before then voting was a very public business and potentially dangerous!*

Blackett's Bridge

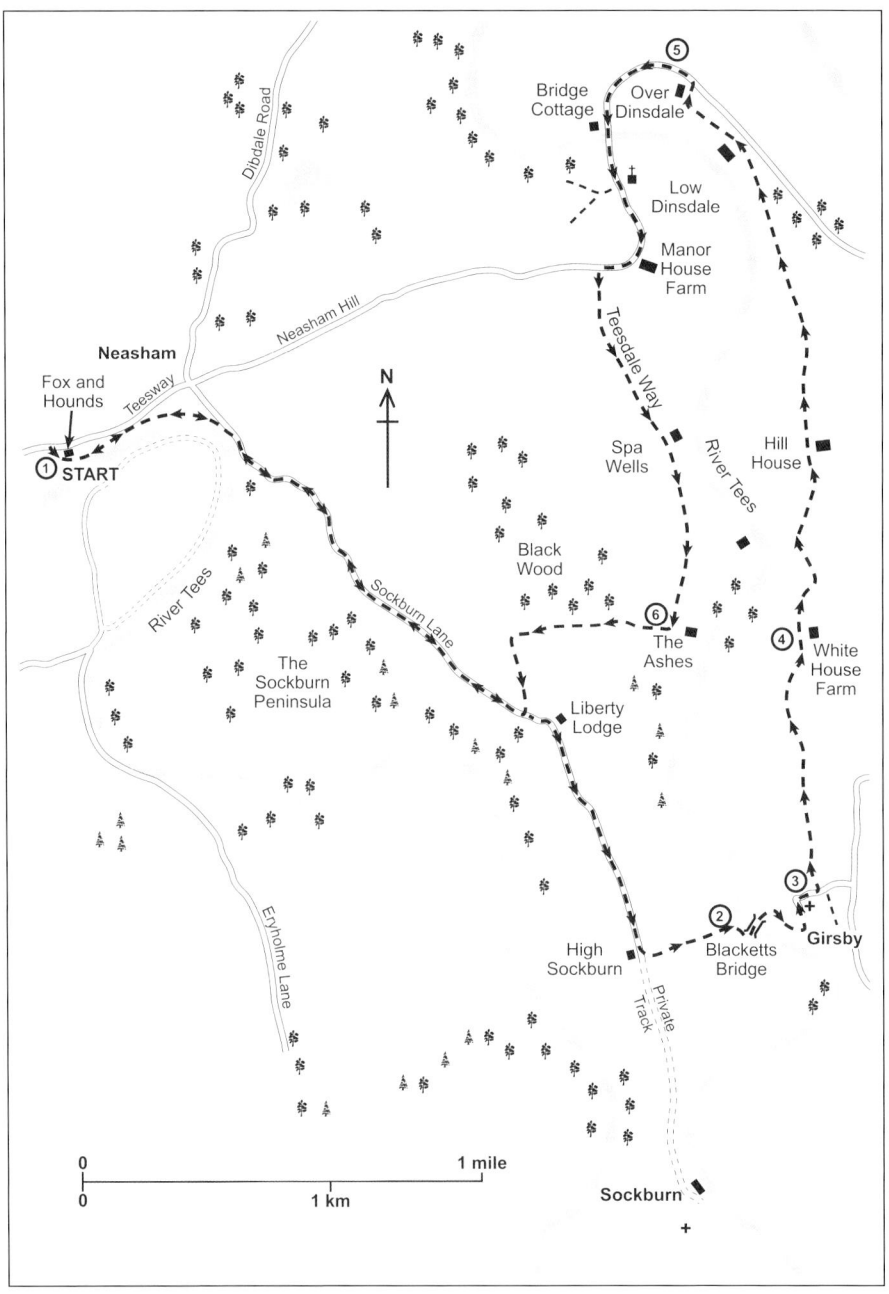

2. Cross the bridge and follow the track uphill and, when it bends left, to Girsby Church. Keep on ahead towards a wide gate and through a wicket gate to its left onto a lane. Turn right up the tarmac lane for a few yards. Opposite the buildings of Church House Farm is a sign 'Teesdale Way. Over Dinsdale 2 miles'. The next couple of miles are almost exactly due north on paths over fields.

The manor, centred on Dinsdale, belonged to the Saxon Siward family, whose descendants built a manor house at Low Dinsdale and a 'motte' castle on the north bank of the Tees at present-day Middleton One Row. Over the centuries the Siward family changed their name to Surtees, which is Norman French for 'on Tees', and produced several well-known family members including Bessie Surtees, who famously eloped from a window along the Quayside at Newcastle with young John Scott, the future Lord Eldon and Tory Lord Chancellor.

3. Follow the line of this signpost straight over the arable field (the farmer leaves a clear route across this and the next fields). At the far side go through a hedge gap (marked with a post although the waymark is missing). Keep ahead and then through a wide gap in the next facing hedge. Keep on ahead to a track junction where you keep on to go through a wide gate then down a path through scrubland and a young plantation. This can be muddy and slippy. The path rises to go through a fence gap into the next field (waymarked). Keep straight on over the field. Cross a stile in the facing hedge. Now cross the next field diagonally to the right towards White House Farm. Go through a hedge gap and keep on over the gravel drive of the farm.

4. Just past the farm go through a gap in a hedge corner. Now follow the left field edge. Don't go through a wide gap in the next facing hedge but bear right to reach a signed metal wicket gate. In the next long field bear slightly right diagonally and follow the line marked by a couple of posts to exit near the field corner by a wicket gate next to a wide field gate. Follow the left fence to cross a stile next to a wide gate and keep on ahead past Hill House on the right and go through another wicket gate. Now keep on ahead past a single tree. At the far side there is (was) a fallen tree and the waymarked wicket gate is beyond it (you may need to bend or crawl!). Continue on over the next arable field. At the next facing hedge go through a wide field gate (fallen?) and follow a, potentially very muddy, woodland path. At the woodland edge go through a gap by a stile and keep on over the next field.

Go through a wide gate near a house and on ahead through a wicket gate. Exit this stretch down a gravel track and through a wide gate. Pass cottages on the left and follow the gravel track round to the right past The Grange and The Granary and out onto a road.

5. Turn left (passing Goosepool House) and follow the road round as it bears left to cross a road bridge over the Tees and on past a fine church at Low Dinsdale. Keep on past houses. Just past Manor House Farm and opposite wooden sheds turn right up a concrete drive signed 'Teesdale Way'. Keep on now past a number of very large barns and on along a tarmac lane with a hedge on the left. Pass Spa Wells and keep on to reach The Ashes.

Low and Over Dinsdale are opposite each other across the Tees and derive their name from a personal name such as 'Dicten' or 'Dictune' while the suffix 'ale' is from the Old English 'hal' which means a meadow. So this was the meadow land of Dicten but his name has been corrupted into a shorter version. Tees is another of the many British river names and may mean

St. John the Baptist, Low Dinsdale

boiling or surging water – which it often is! Low Dinsdale was the main settlement in medieval times as it boasts a fine church. According to 'The History and Antiquities of the County Palatine of Durham', 'The Sulphur Well was accidentally discovered in 1789 by labourers employed by the late Mr. Lambton in searching for coal. The men had bored to the depth of seventy-two feet...when the spring burst forth with a tremendous smoke and sulphureous stench. The remarkable qualities of the water attracted the attention of the labourers...and one of them, who had long been afflicted with chronic rheumatism, was perfectly cured by the bath and drinking the water...' Dinsdale Spa was popular well into the 19th century and Dinsdale Station was built to accommodate a trail of sickly visitors.

Spa Wells at Under Dinsdale. Sulphur wells were discovered by labourers in the late nineteenth century

6. Turn right here along a (signed) track through trees and keep on between a little gill and fence. Cross a stile by a double field gate then keep on ahead between Black Wood and a line of saplings. At the field corner cross a stile near another double field gate and walk on for a few yards to join a path along a field edge. Turn left along this to exit onto Sockburn Lane beside the Teesdale Way sign referred to earlier. Now turn right and retrace your steps to Neasham – and the cheerful Fox and Hounds.

CROSSWORD

Across
2. Dragons can twist their bodies into these
4. The name of the village where this walk starts
5. Another word for church
6. Where the worm lived
7. The river in this story
8. The dragon is buried under this

Down
1. The bite and the breath of dragons are this
3. The sword which is still to be seen in Durham Cathedral
5. The surname of the dragon killer
6. Dragons are covered in these

WALK 5
HUTTON RUDBY AND SEXHOW

This time you encounter a monstrous but, thankfully, vegetarian dragon while walking along easy tracks and across quiet fields and miss the chance to touch the skin of a dragon.

THE SEXHOW WORM

Near Hutton Rudby in North Yorkshire is the hamlet of Sexhowe (spelt variously in the past as Sexhowe, Sexou, Saxhow and Saxo). Nowadays it consists of a scattering of farms and cottages and Sexhow Hall which is a farm. It once had a railway station on the line from Stockton-on-Tees to Whitby. Peaceful today it was once the scene of another bloody encounter between man and dragon.

The Sexhow dragon was an abnormally large creature which coiled itself around a hill near to the site of Hutton Rudby Church. There it could gaze across the surrounding farmland and descend occasionally to feast upon milk. Surprisingly vegetarian it was addicted to the constant supply of the milk of nine cows every day. It had no interest in virgins or 'gobbling bairns' and was fairly sedentary in its lifestyle. If it was not fed it devastated the crops with its fiery breath and caused the death of poultry and livestock as well as the great waste of good milk devoted to what was a sort of 'protection racket'. What with one thing and another the farmers had a problem in making ends meet – and there were no subsidies in those days.

Then one day a travelling knight clad in shining armour happened to ride through the hamlet on his questing way. He paused to seek a cooling drink of milk and was told then of the pest which overshadowed life in the vale of the little River Leven. He resolved to remove the menace once and for all.

In fact the beast had not yet received its regular daily tribute and was in an

Sexhow Worm

especially foul mood. Immensely powerful though it was it was also very cumbersome. So although it fought ferociously against the knight he was able to match it with his sharp sword and lance on the back of a specially dragon-trained horse. So round and round he galloped thrusting his lance into its thick carcase wherever he could then darting away before it could close with him.

At last the monster began to weaken from its wounds. This sort of dragon must have not possessed the magical ability to regenerate. That might have been a result of its special milk diet or some sort of flaw in its make-up but it was fortunate for the knight that he was able to wear it down.

Then he leapt down from his steed and drew his sword and approached the still-dangerous opponent. With a number of well placed thrusts into the throat as it reared before him he finally triumphed and it crashed down dead before him!

So the land around Hutton Rudby was now free of the menace which had bedeviled it for so many years and the farmers were now able to prosper once

All Saints Church at Hutton Rudby. According to legend the skin of the Sexhow Worm was kept here

more as their milk sold at the market instead of being used to buy off the threat of death and destruction.

No-one knows to this day who the knight was. After a swift drink of milk given by grateful farmers he rode off again in search of other challenges. After all questing knights also have targets to achieve and appointments to keep!

Interior of All Saints church at Hutton Rudby

Yet the carcase of the dragon remained. And this was skinned by the farmers and the huge skin was hung in the church of All Saints in Hutton Rudby above the Sexhow pew to remind all people of the day when the countryside was freed from the terror which had, for so long, beset it.

NOTES

Indeed there is a curious legend that until the 19th century the skin of the dragon, or at least a portion of it, was still to be seen in the church (*Yorkshire Legends and Traditions* by Rev. Thomas Parkinson (1888)). However there is no sign of it now.

There are other possible connections though. A likely hill for dragon-worms to coil around is the hill known as Whorl Hill which overlooks the site of the former village of Whorlton and whose name suggests that it might have been used for such a purpose. The conifer trees which cover much of it were planted when Queen Elizabeth II came to the throne and in the right light you can see the initials EIIR.

Whorlton also has a castle and a ruined church. The castle dates from the 14th century but there would be one there before that. The gatehouse remains and bears the coats-of-arms of a number of local families. It was here that the arrangements were made for the marriage of Mary, Queen of Scots and Lord Darnley because his father owned it. Not far off is the roofless and ruined Norman church of the Holy Cross. The tower is complete and still has its bell. Inside the church is an unusual stone cross and an oak effigy of a man with a dog at his feet. It's not the knight though – it is probably Nicholas de Meynell who died in 1322.

The hill of the dragon though might be the tree-covered mound near the church and almost opposite Sexhow Hall. It can be seen from the path from the church along the banks of the Leven.

THE WALK

What you need to know	
Distance	5.5 miles
Time	3.5 hours
Map	Ordnance Survey Outdoor Leisure 26 North York Moors; Western Area
Starting point	All Saints' Church, Hutton Rudby. There is a small parking area across the road from the church. Grid Reference NZ469064
Terrain	Mostly riverside paths, tracks and field edges. There are no steep gradients but it can be very muddy in some sections. Mostly old farmland. There are a couple of brief sections of road walking so beware of traffic
How to get there	Hutton Rudby is on the B1365 about 4.5 miles west of Stokesley and three miles to the east of the A19 (T). Post code for SatNav: TS15 0DA (The Bay Horse)
Refreshments	The Bay Horse, the Wheatsheaf and the Kings Head in Hutton Rudby. The Dog and Gun in Potto

1. From the church cross the road bridge over the River Leven then turn left to descend steps. Follow the riverside path. Just past a garden fence corner cross a stile. Keep on with a fence to the right and the river below on the left. Exit via a kissing gate onto a road then turn right up a slope. Just beyond a couple of garages on the left turn left along a public footpath. Cross a stile (barrier). Now follow the left field boundary. There are good views over the Cleveland Hills. Go through a gap in the left field corner and keep on ahead over the next field to descend to cross a metal footbridge into the next field.

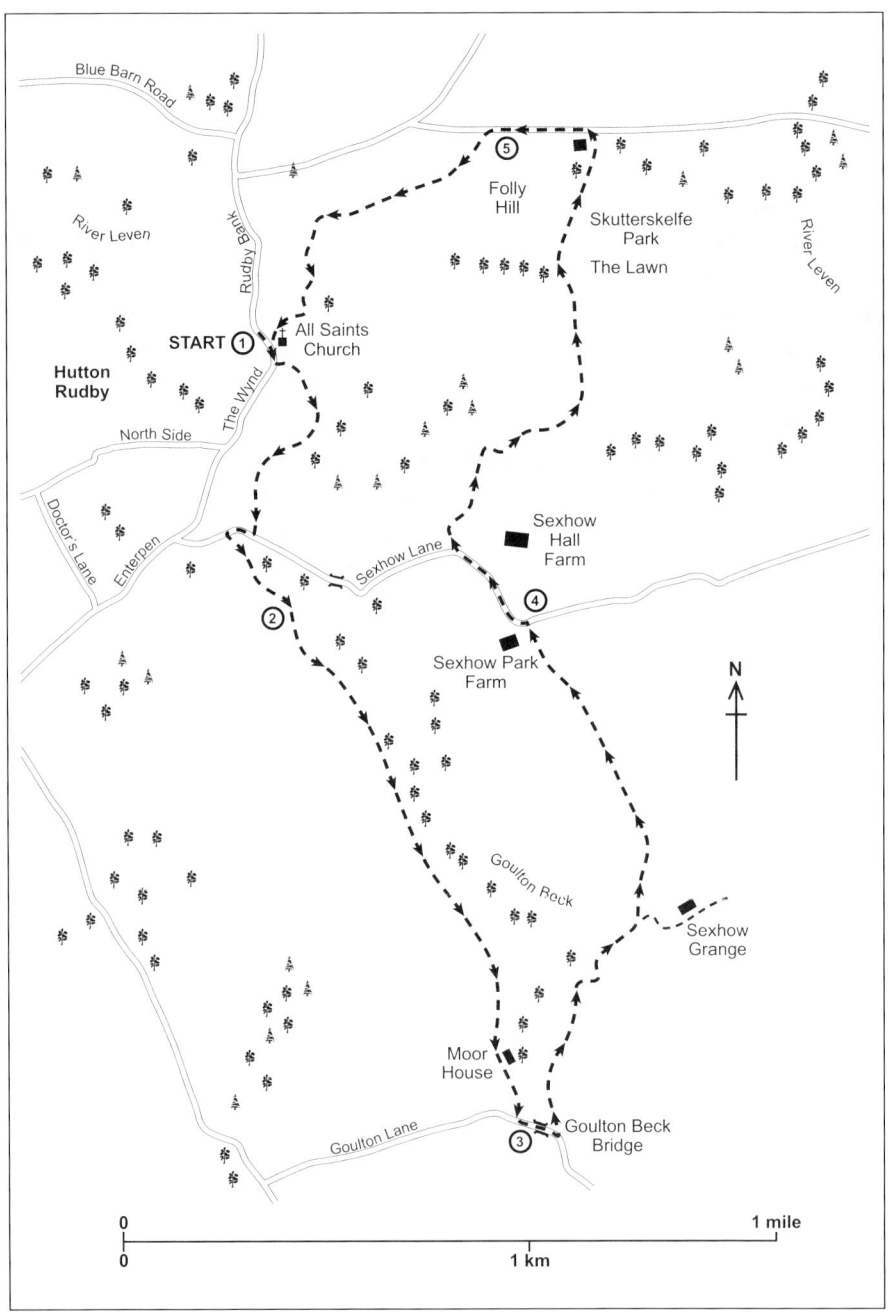

Hutton Rudby has two parts to its name. The second part, 'Rudby' is Viking and means 'Rudi's village'. The first part is Anglo-Saxon and derives from 'Hoh-Ton' meaning 'high farm'. Hutton *is one of the most frequent place names in Yorkshire. Most have a suffix to help distinguish them from one and other.*

2. Turn left then right around the field edge. At the far left field corner don't go through the obvious gap but turn right for a few yards to turn left through a wide gap and keep on straight ahead between trees and into the corner of a small wood where you turn left to cross a footbridge then a stile into a field. Now follow a wire fence on the left uphill. Cross a stile next to a wide field gate and keep on with a fence on the right. Cross a stile on the right through the fence then skirt the corner of Moor House to cross another stile by a wide gate. Now keep on past the farmhouse and over the farm drive to cross another stile into a field. Go ahead and up to another stile to exit the field over an old railway embankment, descending steps and through a gap near a wooden shed. Turn right to cross a stile by a metal gate onto a road. Turn left along this over Goulton Beck bridge. At a sign for Goulton Beck Park Holiday Homes turn left through a kissing gate onto a bridleway.

   Many names for small rivers are specific to geographic location. Beck, burn *and* gill *or* ghyll *are frequent names in the north of England as opposed to* nant *in Wales,* bourne *in the chalk downland of southern England and* brook *in the Midlands, Lancashire and Cheshire.* Stream *is used in Southern England. The words used for such natural features tend to be Celtic in origin*

3. Now follow the gravelled track between old railway viaduct abutments and at a wide gate facing you turn right to follow a wire fence. Follow this (alongside an evergreen hedge) as it bears left then right. Watch out carefully for a muddy path on the left (there is a small metal arrow sign nailed to a tree but easily missed) down to a small beck. Go down this to cross it then go up to follow a track between hedges (can be very muddy). At a wide gate below Sexhow Grange don't go through but go up an enclosed track ahead with a fence on the left and hedge on the right. Go through a gap at the field end and keep on with the hedge on the right into an open area where you keep on towards barns. Pass between these and containers towards Park Farm. The track then splits into two parallel tracks with a line of trees between. Take the left one through a wide gate and on to the farm to exit through a wide gate onto a road.

4. Turn left along the road. At Sexhow Hall Farm, just past the drive end, cross over a (signed) stile on the right then follow a track round right but leave it to cross a good gated footbridge over the Leven. Now head uphill towards a brick structure (pause here to look back at the Cleveland Hills). From the brick building turn right to go through a metal kissing gate and on across the field to a solitary tree where you turn sharp left to a stile. Cross this then go ahead with a metal fence on the right. On the right cross a stile over the fence then turn left and walk on to a shed to go through a metal wicket gate and pass The Lodge onto a road. Keep close in to the side. Turn left up the road and at the top turn left through a wall gap (signed Greenacres/Folly Hill).

Sexhow is claimed to mean either 'Sekk's hill' or 'the six hills'. Leven is a Celtic word. It probably means smooth. Most names of physical features such as rivers, hills and mountains tend to be Celtic and the origin is a matter of conjecture. The Saxons derived their name from a single bladed weapon called a seax so perhaps there might be a clue there ?

5. Don't follow the track but go diagonally right across the field to cross a stile and then pass an isolated gate to cross another stile and go through a metal mesh gate. Now keep on ahead down the field past the left end of battery sheds and through another gate (or the adjacent gap). Keep on to go through another metal mesh gate and on the same line over the next field, past a wartime pill-box, to arrive finally at a footbridge and houses. Don't cross the bridge but turn left with a fence on the right. Cross a substantial stile and descend a (slippy) bank to follow a woodland path. Then cross a footbridge on the right into the church graveyard and walk on up to the church.

One of the major occupations in Hutton Rudby was flax spinning and weaving. Most of the flax was imported from the Baltic. This linen industry became more and more important, until by 1831 the village had more weavers for its size than any other village in the North Riding of Yorkshire. In 1834 a power-driven spinning mill was established alongside the Hutton corn mill, beside the bridge over the Leven. From then on this was the centre of the village weaving, and for over 70 years sailcloth was made here, first by water and then by steam-power. Weaving villages were quick to follow the teachings of John Wesley the founder of Methodism. He visited Hutton Rudby a dozen times between 1759 and 1790, writing in his diary in 1766 that the Methodist society here was 'the largest in these parts and the most alive to God'.

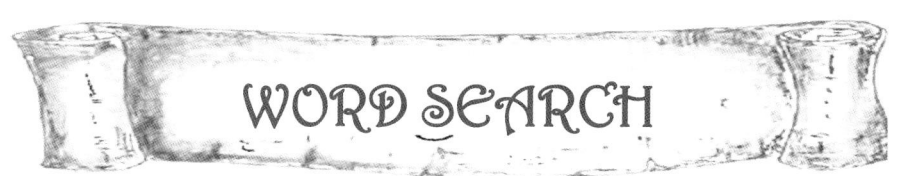

WORD SEARCH

a	a	g	s	m	y	a	v	d	x	y	v	n	x	p
p	r	r	p	e	d	n	l	c	p	b	e	e	o	j
j	m	s	u	i	x	u	v	j	y	d	g	v	z	p
g	o	h	z	l	f	h	q	u	i	u	w	e	z	s
o	u	q	n	a	v	n	o	s	g	r	n	l	m	u
e	r	u	r	d	j	j	y	w	v	n	u	d	v	h
d	c	m	b	h	i	r	c	l	u	o	l	h	j	q
c	e	n	t	z	t	k	j	q	q	t	s	t	o	p
r	s	q	a	n	d	e	e	t	s	t	z	t	i	l
p	w	i	u	l	q	n	s	e	m	u	i	s	f	k
g	i	o	w	l	v	k	s	y	e	h	t	g	l	o
z	c	r	e	g	e	n	e	r	a	t	e	i	v	i
n	w	h	f	l	l	s	v	h	h	l	m	w	k	n
g	e	w	h	u	f	w	g	e	t	m	o	v	d	o
b	k	f	x	p	o	c	u	p	t	v	q	e	a	l

armour
countryside
farmer
huttonrudby
lance
leven
milk
regenerate
sexhow
steed

WALK 6
LIVERTON AND HANDALE

A working class and untrained Teesside lad rather than a 'toff' knight does the job against a hypnotist worm here in a land of rapidly diminishing women. The walk itself follows easy field paths and woodland tracks.

THE HANDALE SERPENT

No two dragon stories are completely alike. Many of them have features in common of course – good story tellers will always recognize some embellishment which could be comfortably lifted from another tale and deposited in their own repertoire! The Handale Serpent does share features with other dragon stories. However, what is unusual about it is that the dragon killer in this case is just an ordinary young man. Usually they are knights of noble birth on quest or 'returning from foreign wars'. The Handale hero though, according to some versions, is no such 'toff' but just a local peasant youth. With a name like 'Scaw' he would hardly pass for a member of the gentry or a knight of the Round Table would he?

As usual though the story begins with a 'loathly worm'. North Yorkshire seems to have had plenty of these. This one lived in a lair at Handale, south of Loftus. It preyed on the land between Handale and Loftus. In particular it seems to have been attracted by young maidens whom it seized and took back to its home to consume at its leisure. According to some accounts it actually hypnotized them with its 'great big goggly eyes' and enticed them to the lair. The result of this was a growing shortage of young women in the area and a severe gender gap! Naturally the local villagers were very concerned about this decimation of the maidens of Loftus and environs but they were terrified of the dragon and unable to help themselves.

Then one lucky day there arrived a strong and handsome young man called Scaw. He was on the lookout for a wife but soon heard that he was unlikely to find one in this area since they were disappearing one after another to the lair of the dragon. Many people would just move on to somewhere else like Whitby perhaps but Scaw was not that sort of person. He resolved to stay and to seek out the menace and deal with it.

So the first thing to do was to get the right equipment. Most dragon-killers would have their own but not Scaw. In those days a full set of armour and a sword would be worth the equivalent of ten or fifteen years of the average peasant income. Perhaps he borrowed sword and armour? He could manage without a horse one supposes because the area was heavily wooded and he would have to dismount to fight. Anyhow he was equipped from some source or another – otherwise the story could not proceed.

Then he walked from Loftus to Handale – a walk of three or four miles and not easy to accomplish clad in plate armour on a warm day, and with a shield and a sword of over a yard in length. According to some accounts his appetite for danger was whetted by the news that the most recent victim of the beast was the daughter of the local Lord of the Manor, Richard de Beckwith. Indeed this had been within only a day or two of his arrival in the area.

So Scaw moved on to find the lair which was a woodland cave. Now there is still woodland in the area and in those days it will have been a good deal thicker and impenetrable in places. Nevertheless he persevered and made his way through the trees until at last he arrived at Handale where there is a small valley with wooded banks. There he could now see a rocky cliff and a large cave at the base of it. From the terrible noise coming from the cave he knew the dragon lay within. Now he needed a plan!

After all Scaw was not a regular dragon killer, and nor was he accustomed to using sword or armour. However he was cunning and fleet of foot and could take advantage of the woodland cover.

So he approached the cave and made as much noise as possible – shouting and clashing his long sword on his shield. The dragon was infuriated by this intrusion and, spitting flames and roaring, it came from the innermost interior of its cave and out into the sunlight.

What followed was a race between Scaw and the great clumsy beast. Rather than challenge it to a straight contest the nimble Scaw moved quickly through the trees and behind boulders and round and round the dragon. It lumbered

Handale Serpent

around after him and with its huge body thrashed and beat down the weaker trees and undergrowth. But he was too quick for it. All the time he taunted it and dodged in and out to bewilder it all the more.

More than once the flames breathed by the dragon came close to Scaw and he was almost blinded by the black smoke and poisoned by the venomous breath. Without the suit of armour he would have been killed and shriveled up and blackened by the combination. Of course the heat inside the protective shell was almost unbearable. Naturally he began to tire. He had to find a moment and a vulnerable point in the skin of the beast – the eyes or the throat. Eyes would be best but only a small target. He did manage to slash at the tough hide of the dragon but only a deep thrust would do the job. Using a sword was very new to a peasant like Scaw. Knights would have trained in the use of swords and the wearing of armour since the age of seven or eight. Even so he was learning quickly.

Then at last as he turned round the edge of a great moss covered boulder he tripped on a tree root, and suddenly poised above him was his opponent which now had him at its mercy. With the last of his strength Scaw turned and raised himself and thrust his long, double edged blade upwards and into the less well defended throat of the awful creature. For what seemed a long time, but will have been only a few seconds in reality, there was a silence and the world appeared to stand still. Then with a great crash the dragon fell down dead.

Scaw managed now to recover his strength and to drink from the little burn in the valley bottom. He cut the awful head of the dragon from its stinking carcase. Then he stumbled into the darkness of the lair recoiling in horror at the sight of the bones and rotting flesh of the previous victims of the dragon. Then he saw, cowering in the depths of the cave, the daughter of de Beckwith. Gently and with reassurances he took the poor girl by her hand and led her out into the sunlight and back to Loftus to reunite her with her family.

So the story ends happily. But more was to come. He married the girl at a great wedding party attended by people from far and wide, so great was the renown of this humble young man and so relieved were they to be freed from the menace of the Handale Serpent. Then when Sir Peter died Scaw inherited all of his wealth and lands and he lived, with his lovely wife, for many years.

NOTES

Technically Handale is now within the entirely artificial modern county of Cleveland. Boundary reformers are no admirers of dragon legends. Nevertheless it is on the northern edge of the boundary of the North Yorks Moors National Park. It is not actually far from Loftus or the main Moors road to Whitby with its noisy holiday makers but still seems remote. It is at the head of a tree-lined pleasant valley called Grenedale (or 'Grindale' or 'Grendale'). A small stream runs through a picturesque ravine and on to Loftus and the Kilton Beck. In fact, there is no village of Handale but there is the quiet village of Liverton near by.

In 1830 sixteen human skeletons were found at the priory. The exact details of what was found is slightly unclear and differs depending upon the source you read. Essentially though the finds included a stone coffin, a stone pedestal of a font or cross and a sword. The skeleton with the sword was, naturally, associated with Scaw. One source suggested the stone coffin lid had a sword carved on it and 'snake slayer'. For many years it attracted sight-seers but the coffin is now gone. However an area of woodland is still named Scaw's Wood, and marked as such on the maps of H.M. Ordnance Survey. So what better proof could you possibly want of this remarkable story and the triumph of the common man over dreadful adversity?

The story is an old one. Writing in 1888, Rev Thomas Parkinson in his *Yorkshire Legends and Traditions* gives an account of the death of the Handale Serpent which is the basis for this one. He refers to its peculiar and disturbing ability to mesmerise its prey. 'In ancient times these quiet woods were infested by a huge serpent, possessed of most singular fascinating powers, which used to beguile young damsels from the paths of truth and duty, and afterwards feed on their dainty limbs....'

The Beckwiths of Handale Abbey were probably the family associated with Beckwith which is two miles south west of Harrogate. Scaw did very well for himself indeed. It was the ancient seat of the family, which owned property here until 1753.

THE WALK

What you need to know	
Distance	6 miles
Time	3.5 hours
Map	Ordnance Survey Explorer OL27 North Yorks Moors Eastern Area
Starting point	Liverton Village Hall. Grid Reference NZ711159
Terrain	Bridleways, footpaths and sections of roads. In Loftus the route follows the busy A174 briefly. Mostly field edges and woodland tracks and paths. A couple of steep gradients.
How to get there	Liverton is 2.5 miles south of Loftus via the B1366. Postcode for SatNav: TS13 4TB (The Waterwheel). The Liverton Village Hall is just a few hundred yards north of The Waterwheel
Refreshments	The Waterwheel in Liverton. The Arlington Hotel is on the route in Loftus

1. From the village hall walk south to the intersection of the road with Moorsholm Lane. Turn left along the bridleway (ie. along the lane). Go through a wide gate and on between paddocks. Keep on between ponds to the left and right and past gallops. Start to descend Handale Bank passing a weighbridge. You approach a complex of barns and silos and other buildings. Just beyond a brick building turn right at a bridleway sign (diverted route) through a wide field gate. Keep slightly leftwards over the field to a fence corner then turn left to go through a wide gate. Keep on down alongside the fence on the right passing through another wide gate then down to the field corner to pass through a wicket gate. Now follow a narrow (muddy) path. At the bottom cross the footbridge over the Handale Beck.

Liverton is a planned, medieval, upland village of probable 11th century date. The medieval village plan consisted of two rows of farmsteads facing each other across an open green and centred on the crossroads formed by

The Water Wheel Inn at Liverton

> Liverton Road with the lanes to Handale and Moorsholm. Each property had a strip of intensively cultivated land (garth or burgage plot) to the rear. The usual pattern for villages of this type is for the rows of burgage plots to end at a back lane. In Liverton they end at streams.

2. Ignore a wicket gate on the left. Keep on up a stony woodland path between a hedge and narrow gully. Go through a wicket gate at the top. Keep on along the side of a fence past a wicket gate. Bear round the edge to go through a wide gate and onto a gravel track. Stay with this and ignore a wicket gate on the right. Keep on between barns and farm buildings (Handale) and round to the right – still on a wide track. Continue on through a wicket gate by a field gate. Go through another wide gate into Warren Wood. At the woodland end and a junction of track and road turn right along the quiet lane. Keep on between an avenue of deciduous trees. Then just before a road junction look left for a gap blocked to vehicles by rocks but unsigned.

Handale Abbey Farm lies on the site of an old Cistercian Abbey. In 1133 a small Benedictine priory of nuns was founded there by Richard de Percy. It later became Cistercian. In the 16th century when it was dissolved it passed to the Beckwiths. From them it eventually passed on to a Mr. Sanderson of Staithes and then the Stephenson family. There is very little left of Handale Priory itself. For a while the buildings were used for the manufacturing of cotton which stopped in the late 18th and early 19th century with the lack

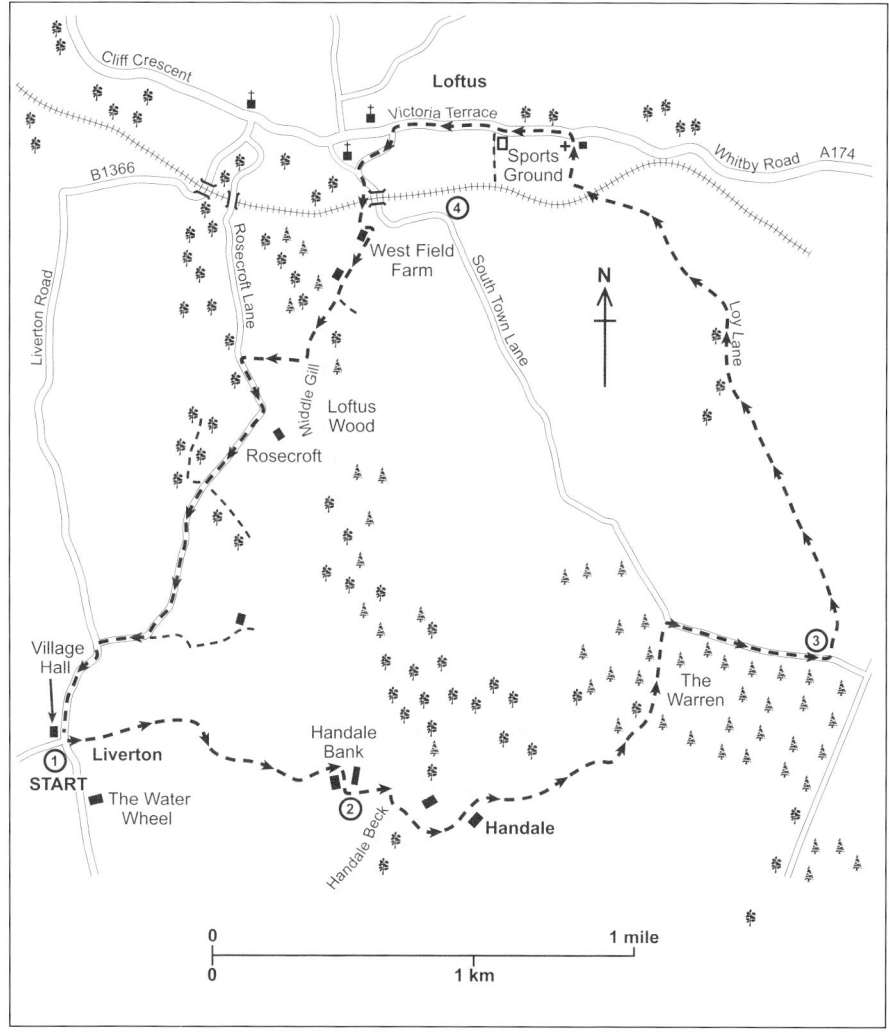

of demand during the Napoleonic Wars. In 1846 the remaining buildings were demolished with the stone being used for the nearby Handale Abbey Farmhouse and Handale Abbey Walled Garden.

3. Turn left down Loy Lane. The easy, pleasant path follows the woodland edge with hedging on the right. Eventually the hedge is lost and the path begins to skirt round cultivated fields. Just keep on. Cross a track and then the path continues between hedges again. You pass allotments and a small cemetery on the left. Cross a bridge across the railway from the Cleveland Potash Mine at Boulby. Keep on through the cemetery and finally exit onto the A174. Turn left along the Whitby Road. Pass Glenfield Terrace and Windsor Terrace. Pass the Loftus Cricket and Athletics Club. Then continue along Arlington Street. Watch out for Dam Street on the left. Turn left along Dam Street following a little channelled stream. Keep on by (or over) a footbridge then on under a railway bridge and up to a road junction.

Loftus is recorded in Domesday Book. The name derives from Laghthus *meaning* low houses. *The Loftus area has been inhabited since at least the 7th century. The only known Anglo-Saxon royal burial site in north-east England is near Loftus. The Methodist preacher John Wesley is*

Loftus North Road c. 1900

known to have preached in Loftus. More recent history is dominated by the ironstone mining industry, and many inhabitants that live in Loftus can trace lineage back to ironstone miners. Imperial Chemical Industries (ICI) started producing potash at Boulby in 1973. Because of its depth, Boulby Mine is used to house the ZEPLIN-III dark matter detector.

4. Turn right past a small terrace of cottages on the right and past Westfield Farm on the left. Keep on round on a lane then earth track. At a hedge gap on the left cross a stile and turn right past Rose Cottage (with its impressive topiary). Keep on ahead then down a severe slope. At the bottom cross a stile and then a new footbridge over Waytail Beck and into Loftus Wood. Turn left along the woodland path and go up a flight of steps to cross an awkward stile. Follow the left field edge to exit onto a quiet lane via a stile. Now turn left and walk on along Rosecroft Lane. This descends and rises. Pass the drive to Blue House Farm on the left and keep on to the junction with Liverton Road at the village sign.

p	j	t	h	q	u	r	f	m	w	d	p	z	v	s
g	b	c	x	o	u	c	j	n	a	s	y	e	b	c
s	o	h	l	o	b	l	v	k	u	i	n	u	x	a
h	y	c	m	d	e	i	z	r	f	o	d	q	q	w
m	a	r	b	g	c	b	h	k	m	q	w	e	g	s
s	a	s	c	w	k	p	x	o	u	e	n	s	n	p
d	u	a	q	v	w	f	u	e	l	a	d	n	a	h
o	v	t	y	i	i	s	o	g	q	d	u	v	m	e
e	i	q	f	z	t	g	r	b	m	q	d	c	q	r
n	v	a	d	o	h	n	e	l	s	n	j	p	e	j
o	f	x	a	z	l	g	n	c	d	a	r	m	v	s
g	q	u	n	x	k	p	x	s	m	c	p	d	s	c
a	p	o	v	f	h	o	r	h	k	e	d	f	u	z
r	k	n	i	g	h	t	f	s	l	w	d	p	d	s
d	w	k	w	r	d	t	t	f	b	r	i	x	s	l

armour

beckwith

cave

dragon

handale

knight

loftus

maiden

scaw

venomous

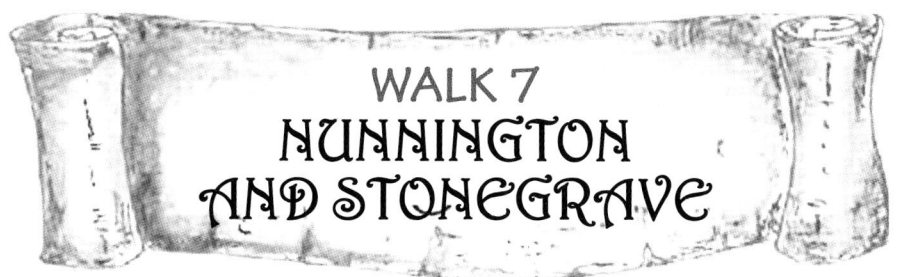

WALK 7
NUNNINGTON AND STONEGRAVE

There is no happy ending in this story. Everyone dies! However, you can console yourself by enjoying a lovely view from Caulkely's Bank in between field edge and riverside walking.

THE NUNNINGTON WORM

The little village of Nunnington is nowadays a very pretty, quiet village just over the southern edge of the North Yorkshire Moors National Park boundary. Its old yellow limestone, red pan-tiled houses and its location on the banks of the River Rye make it attractive to tourists nowadays. Yet according to legend it was once the scene of a very bloody encounter between a monstrous dragon and a famed knight.

This story begins quite precisely on the 11th June, the day of St. Barnabas, some time before the conquest of England by the Normans. The day was also Mid Summer Day (in the 18th century calendar changes would turn the 11th June to the 24th June over night, and it is the 24th June which is Mid Summer Day now). This was the day when the folk of the countryside celebrated the gathering in of the hay. St. Barnabas had been a farm labourer so he was the appropriate patron saint.

In Nunnington on that day as usual there was a great bonfire on the hill top near where the church stands today. The villagers from Nunnington and surrounding settlements gathered around and enjoyed music and dancing and general merry-making. The high point of the occasion was the crowning of the Barnaby Queen. The most beautiful maiden of the area would be selected and then transported on a hay cart from near the River Rye up to the bonfire. The load of new hay on which she sat was the symbolic final load of hay. The cart and horse were decorated and escorted by a procession of young bachelors.

The Nunnigton Worm

The maiden chosen on this occasion was fifteen years of age and she was called Frances Mortain. She wore a white dress and her fair hair was adorned with a crown of summer flowers. In her hand she carried a posy of flowers. As she approached the top of the hill and the bonfire the villagers clapped and sang.

However to the horror of the assembled crowd just as the maiden approached the air was filled with the sound of great wings as a monstrous flame-spewing dragon descended. They screamed and fled in all directions leaving only young Frances perched on her hay throne. In seconds the beast wrapped its oily coils around her and carried her off to a lair on the summit of Loschi Hill between Stonegrave and Nunnington. There the maiden would have been consumed by the dragon if it had not been for a remarkable stroke of luck.

At just that moment there arrived a famed warrior called Sir Peter de Loschi. He was a knight of the Round Table of the great King Arthur. He had a great reputation as the killer of Saxon enemies of his king, and the successful antagonist of a veritable menagerie of fearsome creatures including a lion, dragons and even a hippogriff! However even questing knights take time off and Sir Peter had chosen to return to his home village and to relax, away from the perils of the land of Camelot. So, with his faithful hound, he arrived at Nunnington in the nick of time.

It may be that Sir Peter employed the same sort of protection as did the young John Lambton of Wearside – that is to say a suit of armour studded with blades – to counteract the regenerative powers of dragons. Or perhaps not! Interesting details have a habit of being transmitted between stories to increase their effect. Anyhow Sir Peter had his hound, his horse and a sword made of the same metal as the fabulous Excalibur of his lord King Arthur. So off rode he to Loschi Hill watched by the villagers.

The dragon saw him coming and attacked him. Peter was fast though. He slashed at the beast with his great sword and leapt away from its massive jaws. Meanwhile the loyal hound sought to bite the creature and help his owner. So the struggle went on and, try as he might, Sir Peter could not kill the dragon because no sooner had he driven his sword into its flesh than the cuts healed. Hour after hour the fight went on and the knight began to tire.

Then the tide began to turn. As greasy gobbets of dragon skin and flesh were cut away the hound began to seize them before the wound re-healed and then carried them away. The dragon roared with fury and with pain. As it suffered it became ever more venomous and threatening and began to attack the plucky dog as well. Yet every time the knight was able to slice away a section of the body of the dragon his helper gripped it between his teeth and carried it off. Unable now to heal itself the tormented monster began to weaken and suffer from the blows of the magical sword. Finally only the loathsome head remained, and this was carried away to Nunnington as a trophy by the gallant fighting dog.

Sir Peter now examined the lair to search for fair Frances. But she was no more. She had perished as had all of the previous victims of the dragon. So Sir Peter turned to limp back to the village but sadly, as he approached, he was greeted by his joyful hound whose frantic licks were laced with the poison of the flesh of the dragon. Within a few seconds Sir Peter fell dead, and so did his poisoned hound. They were later buried together.

To this day visitors can see for themselves the effigy of Sir Peter and his hound lying in the church of All Saints and St. James and think of that great fight on the day of St. Barnabas.

NOTES

The death of every participant is certainly a novel ending!

The restored 13th century church does indeed contain a stone effigy of a knight with a lion at his feet. The

The church of All Saints and St. James dates from the 13th century

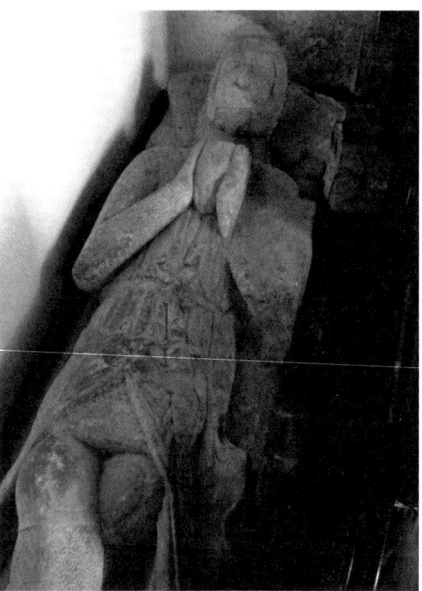

Supposedly the effigy of Peter de Loschi. In fact a case of mistaken identity

carving actually represents Sir Walter de Teyes, Lord of Stonegrave Manor (born 1297). Walter served both King Edward I and King Edward II, who, in 1309, made him joint Governor of York. Dying in 1325 he was buried in All Saints Church, Nunnington. You need a good stretch of imagination though to turn these into Sir Peter and the flesh-carrying hound. Presumably it was a huge Talbot Hound, a mastiff-type which is now extinct. You'd need a big dog to fight a dragon though. A fragment of a tenth-century stone cross does show a part of a dragon.

There is indeed a prominent hill to the east called Loschi Hill. The field immediately to the south of the church is known as Worm Field – and there the pieces of the dragon body were buried supposedly. The name of the maiden gives some precision to the story, although the surname Mortain is actually of Norman French origin.

THE WALK

What you need to know	
Distance	7 miles or 4.25 miles
Time	4 hours or 3 hours
Map	Ordnance Survey Outdoor Leisure 26 North York Moors Western Area covers most but not all of this. A small section at Stonegrave is on the Ordnance Survey Explorer 300 Howardian Hills and Malton
Starting point	The village of Nunnington. You can park in a lay-by next to 'Gallery Beyond' just a few yards to the west of the church where this walk commences. Grid Reference SE665792
Terrain	Mostly along field edges. A large section is along the banks of the quiet River Rye but the most spectacular section is along Caulkleys Lane and over Caulkleys Bank (alternatively spelt as Caulklass.) There are a few short sections of road walking. At the height of summer the field edges can be very heavily overgrown and tripping is an ever present hazard

How to get there	Nunnington is 6 miles south east of Helmsley. Taking the A170 from Helmsley turn onto the B1257 then after 4 miles turn off along a minor road to Nunnington. Postcode for SatNav: YO62 5US (The Royal Oak Inn)
Refreshments	The Royal Oak Inn in Nunnington

1. From the church turn right to go down the main street of Nunnington. At the bottom turn right along Low Street. Walk on past Nunnington Studios then a small chapel and arrive at a road. Across the road is Nunnington Hall. Turn right for a few yards past Nunnington Village Hall on the left. At a fence corner cross a stile and turn left to follow a fence on your left. Keep ahead past a large house and on to cross a stile next to a wide field gate. Keep on over the field to cross another stile next to a wide gate near Mill Farm.

Nunnington main street. The Royal Oak Inn is on the left. The Rye is at the bottom of the street

The first Nunnington Hall was mentioned in the thirteenth century and the site has had many different owners

> The first Nunnington Hall was mentioned in the thirteenth century and the site has had many different owners. The present building is a combination of seventeenth and eighteenth century work. Most of the building seen today was created during the 1680s, when Richard Graham, 1st Viscount Preston, was its owner. Sir Richard Graham of Netherby, who was created Viscount Preston in 1681, was attainted in 1689 for attempting to join James II in France. His lands and property were confiscated, but later returned after he was pardoned.

2. Go on between the buildings, then alongside a high wall on the right and through a wide field gate. Now follow the path along a field edge, then through a gap to continue the next field edge. This stretch can be very overgrown and 'trippy'. At a wide field gate go through a kissing gate and bear slightly left to ascend a slight rise to a fence corner. Follow the fence on your left and keep on through a kissing gate and on along the field edge path with the Rye more visible. Go through another kissing gate and on along the river edge for a few yards to exit onto a road via another kissing gate.

3. Turn right up the road here passing West Ness Hall on the right. Just past a road junction turn right up a signed, hedge-lined track. Keep up past a barn on the left and on ahead to cross a track and continue on the same line. This is Caulkleys Lane and it affords splendid views over the Howardian Hills. You join a gravel track. Turn left briefly then right to continue on the grassy track which is rising steadily. You will arrive at a perfectly placed stone bench beside a trig point. Soon after cross a road (The Avenue) and keep on along the track now signed to Stonegrave. After a short while there is another track leading off to the right. This would take you directly back to Nunnington. Otherwise just continue.

The Howardian Hills take their name from the Howard family who still own local lands. They are located between the Yorkshire Wolds, the North York Moors National Park and the Vale of York and are a designated Area of Outstanding Natural Beauty. The Howardian Hills form 79 square miles of well-wooded, undulating countryside

4. The track becomes a well pounded tractor way. Just keep ahead. When it turns right keep on ahead along a grassy track. Keep left to go through a wide gate (signed) and then keep on down a curious sunken way with views over Stonegrave. Keep on ahead where the track is joined by another from the left. Then exit across a stile by a wide field gate and walk down to join the busy road. Visit the very interesting Stonegrave Minster but then return to this spot to keep on along the road westwards.

Stonegrave simply reflects the fact that there was a stone quarry there ie. stan *or* stane = stone *and* graef = quarry. *Stonegrave Minster was established before 757 AD. It was probably founded by a King of Northumberland. Part of the west wall may date from Saxon times. The church was virtually rebuilt in the 12th century. Then in 1863*

Stonegrave Minster viewed from the east

97

Victorian 'restoration' took out the medieval interior. The effigy of William Thornton (d. 1330) is unusual in being a civilian with legs crossed. The church contains fragments from four Saxon standing crosses, together with an almost complete cross. The great cross itself has no parallel in Ryedale.

5. At a signpost on the right for 'Nunnington 1.5 miles' turn up a clear track which winds round upwards and right and alongside woodland. Then it levels out. Keep on to reach a gap in the hedge and a fallen signpost (at the time of writing). Turn left now and follow the track round the field edge passing another marker post. The track doubles back but just follow it steadily on through a wide gap in a hedge and on alongside a hedge on the right. Keep on through another wide gap and continue. You arrive at a minor road – Nunnington is along to the right.

6. Turn left along the road then very soon at double field gates, and a sign for Harome cross a stile and follow a track down on the right side of a hedge. Keep on through a gap between field hedge ends and follow the winding track left then right between fields. Then at the corner of woodland follow a sign for Nunnington on a field edge path with trees to the left. At a field corner go left through a gap and across an earth covered culvert. Turn right now to follow the field edge path alongside a ditch. At the next field corner turn right to cross a footbridge and now turn left alongside the tranquil River Rye. Continue on past the end of a closed and dangerous footbridge. Keep on past a marker post into another field. Pass the end of another bridge to arrive at a wicket gate. Go through and keep on across a field with a bank on your right side. Go on through a gap/wicket gate. Finally you reach a kissing gate/wide field gate which admits you to the bottom of the main street of scenic Nunnington beside a wide footbridge. The Royal Oak Inn is just up there!

Nunnington's name has nothing to do with nuns but is a three-part name meaning the settlement of the people of Nunna ie. tun = settlement, ing(a) = folk or people and Nunna. The rather exotic sounding name Harome simply means rocks/stones ie. haer = stone and um = of so this must have lost a word or prefix over time eg. perhaps the place of stones. Rye is a British river-name which probably meant stream. The church of All Saints and St. James dates from the 13th century although parts go back to the 12th century. It was restored in the 17th century then in the late 19th century. Notable features are the unusual font, the effigy of Sir Walter de Teyes (AKA Peter de Loschi) and the plaque on the north wall of the nave commemorating George Jackson who was a very successful jockey

ANAGRAMS

These words have been mixed up.

Can you unscramble

eserfna
noirbef
eyr
preet
nabrabsa
ngnnntunio
raeetgvons
irkoyrseh
slchio
eivsglarl

yorkshire
stonegrave
rye
barnabas
loschi
peter
villagers
bonfire
frances
nunnington

WALK 8
HOVINGHAM AND SLINGSBY

This is a walk of two halves. Field edge and track walking is followed by woodland and the Ebor Way. On the way you encounter a mysterious wizard and a lazy dragon with a novel technique.

THE SLINGSBY DRAGON

It may be seen as suspicious that there are two dragon stories no more than five miles apart in North Yorkshire. Which came first the Nunnington dragon or the Slingsby dragon is not possible to say. Certainly there are records of the Slingsby story as early as 1619 when notes were made on what must have been an older account. Nevertheless there are substantial differences between the two stories.

To begin with the Slingsby serpent dwelt not in a cave or on a hill top like its Nunnington neighbour but in a circular depression by the roadside about half a mile from Slingsby. Some people say it was a gravel pit. It was about ten feet in diameter but the depth was not recorded. This matters because the beast was claimed to be a mile in length, and that would mean an awful lot of body to hide in a hole!

So there it lingered all day waiting for unwary travellers to pass by, or for local and more knowing inhabitants sneaking cautiously past. Then it would leap out from cover and seize its screaming victims which would be duly consumed at its leisure. The toll mounted. This, after all, was quite a busy thoroughfare. The local villagers apparently tried to divert the road away from the hole, and it is claimed that they created a great sweeping curve. If that was the case there is no evidence of it nowadays, and the dragon continued to prey on humanity.

One day Sir William Wyville, reputable exterminator of dragons and such-like, was riding by the depression when he witnessed the abduction of a beautiful local maiden by the loathsome beast. Having wandered from home on some innocent errand or other she had strayed too close to the point of danger and now paid the price. The serpent reached out and grasped her within its coils and then drew her back into its stinking lair.

Sir William did not hesitate. Mounted on his great charger, and with his faithful dog loping along beside him, he charged at the huge beast shouting his war cry. He plunged his lance into its body and it was forced to release the girl from its grasp. She ran to safety bruised and battered. She was to be the only witness of what followed.

Wyville dismounted quickly and drew his great sword. He closed in battle now with the huge dragon and attacked again and again, plunging his long sword into its great body. Time and again he had to leap back away from its great slashing talons and its ghastly teeth. The dog – no doubt a Talbot – leapt in when it could to help its master by biting at it. Together man and dog managed to weaken the monster. Yet Sir William paid a price because he was also tiring.

Eventually though the serpent did fall and Sir William was victorious. He stood with his foot on the head of the dragon and raised his sword in triumph!

However, like Nunnington, there is a sad twist in the tale. The dragon was not yet dead. It had the strength to turn on its tormentors and bite both man and dog with its poisoned fangs. Both fell dead as the dragon also breathed its last.

The story was told by the maiden. She now ran home to give an account of her salvation and of the great deed which she had witnessed by the side of the B1257 (Helmsley to Malton). And so the story was passed down through the generations to the present day.

NOTES

In 1619 the antiquary Roger Dodsworth gave an early account of the dragon: "The tradition is that between Malton and this town there was some time a serpent, that lived upon prey of passengers, and which this Wyvill and his dog did kill, when he received his death-wound. There is a great hole half a mile from the town, round within, three yards broad and more, where the

Slingsby Dragon

serpent lay. In which time the street was turned a mile on the south side, which does still show itself if any takes pains to survey it."

An odd commemoration of this story endures in the decorations around the exterior of All Saints Church. It was rebuilt in 1868 and, typically of these Victorian 'restorations', most of the original church was removed or obliterated. Yet the Church of England is not without a sense of humour. Clearly aware of the story of the dragon it had the east end exterior wall of the church decorated with carved images of a good range of 'fabulous beasts' such as dragons, cockatrices and wyverns. Fascinating!

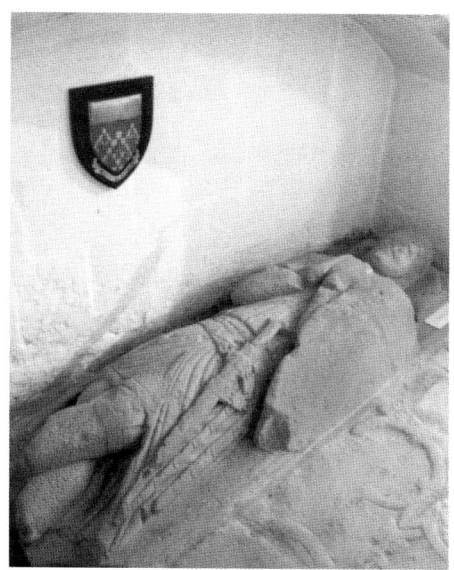

Sir William Wyville is commemorated in effigy inside All Saints Church, with his faithful dog at his feet and his coat of arms above him. However all this demonstrates is that the people of Slingsby had the sense to name their dragon killer after a verifiable figure while those of Nunnington went in for introducing into their story an outsider, and trying to pass off the effigy of someone else as Sir Peter. The Wyvilles had lived in Slingsby since 1215, and it is little wonder that the family and the effigy became part of the legend.

The effigy of Sir William Wyville in all Saint's Church at Slingsby

THE WALK

What you need to know	
Distance	6.5 miles
Time	4 hours
Map	Ordnance Survey Explorer 300 Howardian Hills and Malton

How to get there	Slingsby is south east of Helmsley and stands on the B1257 three miles east of Nunnington. Postcode for SatNav: YO62 4AW (The Lawns lane in Slingsby)
Refreshments	The Grapes in Slingsby and The Malt Shovel and The Worsley Arms Hotel in Hovingham
Starting point	The Church of All Saints at Slingsby. Grid Reference SE695753 for All Saints
Terrain	A section of old railway track then field edge paths between Slingsby and Hovingham. The return from Hovingham is on signed woodland tracks and footpaths and field edges. There are no significant inclines. Sections can be very muddy and wet and can be quite overgrown. There is some slight road walking out of Hovingham and then at the very end into Slingsby. Be very cautious because these are quite busy roads

1. From the church gate turn right to walk along The Lawns. Cross the Lawns Bridge (1935) and keep on along a gravel track. Pass the Lawns Stables then at a cross-tracks near houses keep ahead to cross a stile beside a wide field gate (NB. private drive for Mouse House). Go on ahead. At a house entrance go to the right again to cross a stile and continue on along a hedge-lined path with a paddock over to the right. Cross a little bridge and go through a gate then turn left along a dismantled railway. Keep on past a bench and beyond a wide barrier to reach a crossroads at Greenacres House.

   Slingsby began as the Danish settlement of Eslingesbi or the abode of Eslinc. It appears in Domesday Book in 1086. Slingsby is a pretty village which is easily by-passed. It is on the way to the famous Castle Howard. It is famous for its maypole. The present one is the successor in a long chain throughout the history of the village. It was erected in 1985 and is still used for dancing by children on special occasions.

2. Turn left along Fryton Lane for a few yards then right to resume the same direction along a signed track. Go on between fields on a wide track. This is a pleasant section with a clear view of Hovingham all the way. At a copse in a field corner keep on through a gap passing a four fingered signpost

where a bridleway (to Wath) and footpath cross. Turn left to go through another gap then turn right to follow the left side of a hedge. At a field corner the way is blocked by a ditch. Turn left at a guide post and walk along the field edge to cross a footbridge on the right. Now keep along the right side of a hedge. Go through a gap in trees in the next field corner and keep on ahead to pass to the right of a tennis court and bowling green to exit onto the main road through Hovingham passing the left side of The Malt Shovel. Hovingham Hall is across the road, and guarded by two dragons as well!

All Saints church at Slingsby was rebuilt in 1868

The village is mentioned in Domesday Book. The name is derived from a combination of ing(a) = people, ham = village *and Hofa or Hova which is a personal name. Thus Hovingham was the village where Hofa's folk live. There is evidence of Roman activity around the village which sat on the Malton to Aldburgh road in those times. The village used to be a stop on the Malton & Thirsk branch of the North Eastern Railway. The Hovingham Estate has been in the ownership of the Worsley family for 450 years. Their attractive Palladian home was designed and built by Thomas Worsley between 1750 and 1770. It was the childhood home of Katharine Worsley, Duchess of Kent.*

3. Turn left up the road passing The Worsley Arms Hotel on the left. At a road junction turn off right up the road to Sheriff Hutton/York. Pass The Old Quarry lane on the left but then turn left on a track signed Ebor Way/Terrington. Follow the hedge-lined track and enjoy good views to the north. Keep on into woodland and follow a pleasant signed path. Keep on the signposted Ebor Way past recent woodland clearances and ignore forestry paths to left and right. Eventually you reach a track Y-junction

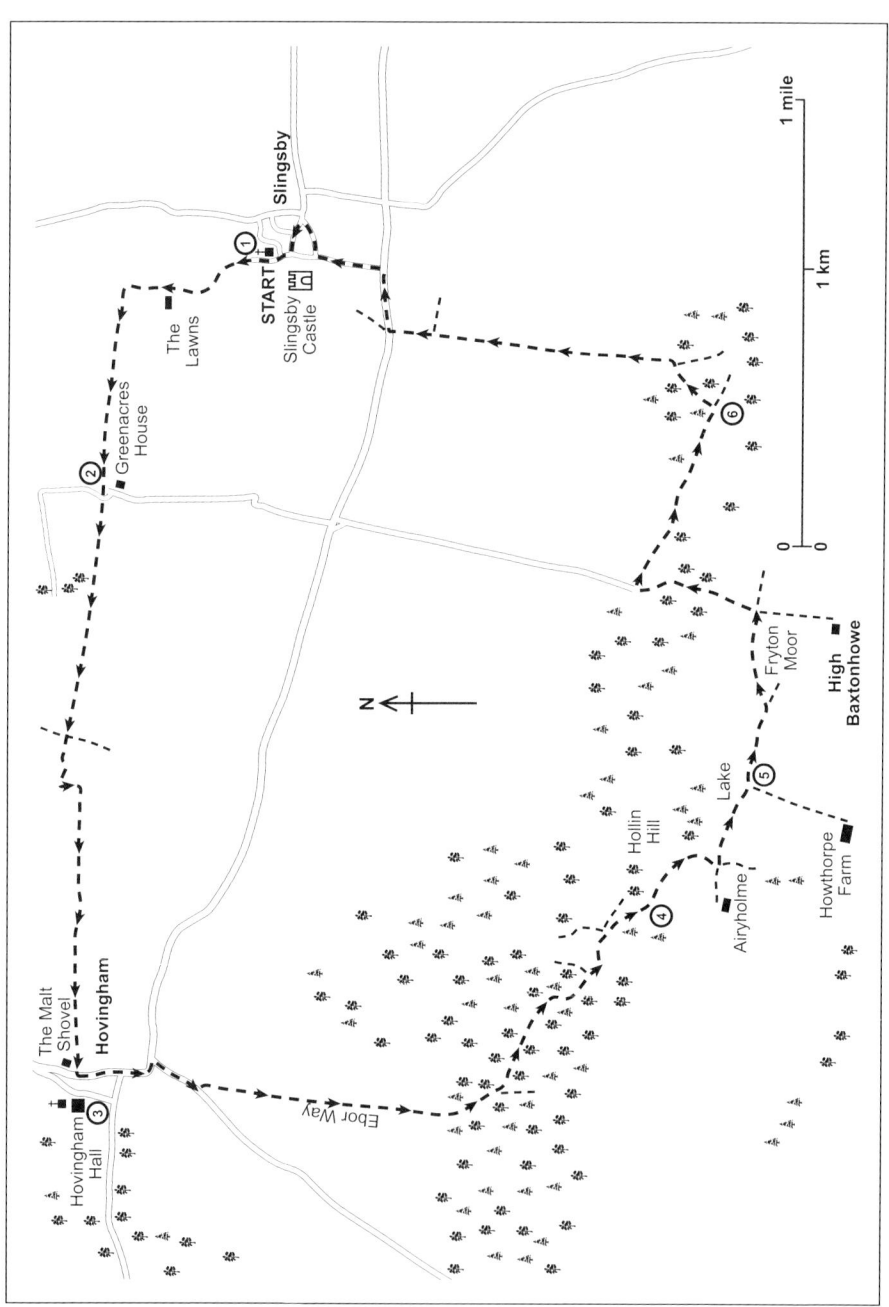

Hovingham Hall was designed and built by Thomas Worsley between 1750 and 1770

just beyond a marker post (with bridleway signs supplemented by a blue arrow on white background). Turn down, ie. left. At a well marked wide field gate go through and follow a grass path ahead over an earth covered bridge and go through a wicket gate. Now follow the field edge round to the left. It enters woodland. Keep on the obvious path which bends right past another post with a blue arrow on white. Follow the clear path as it begins to follow a beck edge. This stretch can be quite thickly overgrown.

The Ebor Way is a 70 mile (112 km) long-distance footpath from Helmsley to Ilkley. It takes its name from Eboracum, the Roman name for York. It connects the Cleveland Way and Dales Way.

4. A three fingered post looms. Follow the sign for the Centenary Way/Ebor Way/Terrington through a field gate, turn left across a bridge/culvert then go through another wide field gate and continue following the Ebor Way indicated on a second, rather superfluous, three fingered post. Keep on along a field edge. You will see Airyholme Farm up on the right but keep on along the field edge until you reach a track leading up to Howthorpe Farm and a guidepost signed Fryton/Ebor Way (and with another finger missing?).

Fryton is probably derived from the Old English for enclosed place. *The name Aireyholme was originally Erghum.* Holme *normally means island or* meander *but in this case it is a corruption in spelling. The suffix* -um *or* -hum *means* at. *Erghum means* 'at the shielings' *and contains the old Irish word* erg *meaning a shepherd's hut or* shieling. *There must have been another part to the name which has been dropped.*

5. Turn left along this to cross a bridge and pass a pond on the left. Go through a double field gate. Now bear right uphill diagonally right to reach a wicket gate in the far corner. Go through and turn right along a track. Follow this between fields. Pass High Burtonhowe Farm on the right and arrive at a very sandy track leading to it. Now turn left down this and then up a bank through trees. Arriving at the signed Centenary Way enjoy a sudden view north towards Fryton. Turn right now following a clear path in woodland edge.

6. At a four fingered post Centenary Way/Hall Moor/Slingsby turn left for Slingsby and follow a grassy path through young trees then older woodland. It comes out at a field corner. Now just keep on down the left field edge alongside a hedge on a wide track passing several wide gaps in the hedge to your left. Keep on past barns, and an impressive collection of tyres. Finally you reach the road where you turn right towards Slingsby (walk along the good grass verge). Turn left down High Street and walk back to the church.

In the background is the mysterious, ivy-covered Slingsby Castle. It is not open to the public. It belonged to Sir Charles Cavendish, the dwarf brother of the Duke of Newcastle who commanded the army of Charles I in the north of England during the Civil War. According to all accounts he was a good man with a 'lovely and beautiful soul'. He was a scientist, philosopher and mathematician. He fought alongside his brother on the fateful field of Marston Moor in 1644, and fled to Europe when all was lost. Their estates were confiscated by Parliament. So there the castle stands today, crumbling and decaying above the village of Slingsby.

WORD SEARCH

q	p	k	n	m	l	d	z	e	b	g	s	a	z	m
i	l	d	a	c	h	j	i	i	e	b	j	e	h	b
q	p	g	t	e	r	k	l	y	c	e	c	e	z	x
d	s	d	u	r	p	j	s	m	q	z	b	y	x	l
s	e	r	p	e	n	t	e	s	t	v	h	n	d	j
w	m	o	d	e	m	e	v	f	l	o	y	b	s	u
o	r	w	z	t	l	o	d	a	f	c	o	m	b	v
y	b	s	g	n	i	l	s	i	y	j	x	f	f	j
m	v	j	n	c	d	p	i	h	a	q	e	j	m	j
w	v	r	l	o	u	u	l	v	t	m	r	y	h	p
r	v	y	t	e	l	p	a	e	y	a	s	y	v	g
s	g	i	q	x	p	a	m	v	v	w	o	w	n	o
h	c	r	u	h	c	s	t	n	i	a	s	l	l	a
j	c	o	r	p	x	q	n	s	y	l	r	z	f	b
l	d	g	r	n	e	n	t	c	h	a	r	g	e	r

allsaintschurch
charger
gravelpit
loathsome
maiden
serpent
slingsby
sword
talons
wyville

WALK 9
RENWICK AND HARESCEUGH

Enjoy a meeting with a highly unusual dragon-type with some particularly unpleasant habits, encounter the Holy Grail and walk along a royal road amidst tracks and field paths in the shortest walk in this book.

THE RENWICK COCKATRICE

In the still, warm, early Autumn of 1733 arrangements were made with a local builder to do basic repairs to the tree-girt, semi-ruined church of All Saints. Sections of plaster had fallen away, there were developing holes in the aged stonework and – worst of all – there was a hole in the roof of the Chancel which afforded a great opportunity to the rain and snow which is so prevalent in this area.

We join our heroes – as they will become – trudging towards the church along the stony track, sweating and panting. Their leader was John Tallentyre of Scalehouses, a local farmer who added to his income with occasional building jobs. Like many builders he had several jobs on, and moved between tasks constantly chased by irate householders for missing appointments. Running alongside him, as always, were his sheepdogs. With him were two assistants – Benedict and Edgar – both of them also part-time labourers on his small farm. On their squeaky wheeled handcart they carried ropes, sections of timber and short ladders which could be erected in a form of (precarious) scaffolding as well as their tools and materials and bread and cheese and ale (vital ingredient on a day such as this).

Little did they know what this particular job would entail!

When the convoy reached the church, which was well known to them of course since it served a very wide area, they paused for breath and to decide how and where to start. It was, of course, obvious that the roof was the priority. The building must be sealed from the elements so that they could deal with the problems of the interior.

Fairly quickly the trio were able to tie together three levels of scaffolding using the short ladders and planks – supported in places by boughs picked from the woodland edge. Not the sort of structure which you or I would put much faith in but our three friends were much used to this sort of life and still bore the old healed fractures and scars to demonstrate it.

Then they began to work. Tallentyre was at the top clearing away debris to get a good base for new timbers to support the roof repair. Meanwhile Benedict and Edgar used a bucket and rope to hoist up tools and materials for him. The loud noise of the disturbed ravens in the surrounding woodland now had added to it the shouting and laughter of the three men as the worked.

Time passed and all went well. Then suddenly the scene changed into one of horror and blood.

One moment Tallentyre was trying to establish a new timber in its place on the Chancel wall and the next he was shouting in fear and waving his arms about above him as a shrieking, hen-headed, black-winged bat-like creature with a long lizard-like tail descended upon him. Of course he had never seen such a creature before. It was, in fact, a cockatrice. They are rare. Not, strictly speaking, a dragon, the cockatrice (or basilisk) is often grouped with dragons. With its loud scream, vicious talons and awful teeth it made up in aggressiveness for its relatively small size. It was just as well that Tallentyre had not looked up and caught the glance of the beast because he would have been turned to stone because, indeed, that is an unusual feature of the repertoire of the cockatrice. As he thrashed around shouting in terror the creature wheeled around and into the Nave of the church. Beneath him were Edgar and Benedict who were only now aware of the peril which faced them all. Quickly they armed themselves with shovels, and prepared to protect themselves against the menace.

Edgar drew from his extensive pocket his large red handkerchief to dry his sweating hands and give him a better grip on the shovel handle. This was a big mistake because the other peculiarity of the cockatrice is its anger at the colour red. Cockatrices are driven demented by red. All that this cockatrice

could see below it on the ground was a flash of red. From a perch at the Nave-end it now swooped down giving its unearthly shriek and making for Edgar. Benedict meanwhile was stumbling up one of the ladders to try and balance himself to swing his shovel down on the creature's head or neck.

Edgar stood no chance. In a confused tangle of thrashing arms and legs and flapping wings Edgar was torn to shreds by the teeth and razor sharp talons. It was over in an instant. So stunned was poor Benedict that he did not even attempt to swing his shovel against the creature. Anyhow he feared that he would hit Edgar in mistake. Now it was his turn. Looking down from his position and unable to do anything to help his friends below Tallentyre saw what happened next.

As the cockatrice turned away from Edgar its fiery red eyes alighted upon the quavering Benedict – and he caught the glance full on in both eyes. Benedict turned to stone. Not gradually but in a trice Benedict turned to stone. At the moment that this happened he was balanced upon the edge of a ladder rung. The stone thing which had been a human turned and fell to the floor and shattered into fragments.

Now the beast turned towards Tallentyre, but he had learnt quickly, and realized the need to avert his eyes from the gaze of the cockatrice. He shaded his eyes with his hand and as he leant to support himself on the makeshift, shaking scaffolding his other hand came into contact with a lengthy and heavy bough of green wood intended to prop up part of the wall. Now Tallentyre might not have known a dragon when he saw one but he knew rowan wood when he saw it. The wood of the humble rowan tree has magical powers. It is proof against witchcraft and makes an effective weapon against such extraordinary creatures as cockatrices. As he heard the flapping wings of the cockatrice he began to thrash around wildly with the bough ahead of him, and immediately he began to feel sharp contact. The shriek of the beast turned to a loud howl and Tallentyre swung his club frantically.

It must have been a lucky hit because suddenly there was silence. Even the ravens were silent. Tallentyre slowly uncovered his eyes and looked down. There beneath him near the mangled remains of Edgar lay the body of the cockatrice.

The rest of the story is straightforward. Local people aroused by the noise made their way to the church and saw a scene of devastation before them.

The carrion body of the cockatrice was hauled away and hurled into a pit and covered with rocks. No-one knows where it is today. The body of poor Edgar was given an honourable burial somewhere in the church grounds but the stone, if there was ever one, has gone. Benedict was nothing more than sharp pieces of stone and these were soon mixed up with debris and lost. You may unknowingly tread on a piece when you visit the church.

And Tallentyre? He did quite well. The Tallantyre family was given hereditary exemption from tithes. He would be able to add an interesting advertising slogan to the side of his cart as well 'John Tallentyre. Builder and Cockatrice Exterminator'!

NOTES

The church has been reconstructed several times and most notably in 1733 and 1845. Some believe the story dates to 1733 but William Hutchinson (1793) dates it to a document of 7 James I (1610) and there is no record of rebuilding then. But the Tallentyre name does first occur in Renwick records in 1608 when a John Tallentyre was included in a list of men entitled to an allocation of timber (for his house). There is nothing to connect to Scalehouses before 1635 when a George Tallentire (sic) was a freeholder (the tithe was held by generations until 1875). But the John Tallentyre of 1608 could have been a freeholder elsewhere. The 1842 Tithe Schedule doesn't include any exemption from tithes. It could have been awarded though and not hereditary.

Apparently there was a claimed sighting of a cockatrice in 1959 – but probably on a walk home after closing time.

THE WALK

What you need to know	
Distance	3.5 miles
Time	2.5 hours
Map	OS Explorer Outdoor Leisure 5 The English Lakes: North Eastern Area and OS Explorer 31 North Pennines Teesdale and Weardale. Most of the route is on the latter

Starting point	Park at the Church of All Saints or roadside parking with consideration for the residents. Grid Reference NY596435
Terrain	Field and woodland paths – sometimes overgrown – and good tracks. There is road walking at the start and the end but on quiet roads. There are a number of stiles and some are not so easy to cross. A couple of moderate inclines
How to get there	Renwick is about eleven miles north east of Penrith and ten miles south west of Alston. Following the A686 south west from Alston turn off for Melmerby after about eight miles down a minor road off to the right from Hartside. Postcode for SatNav: CA10 1JT
Refreshments	None in Renwick. There is the Hartside Top Cafe at the top of the Hartside Pass. Alternatively there is the Robin Hood Inn at Croglin, the Blue Bell Inn at Newbiggin, the Fox Inn at Ousby or the Highland Drove Inn at Great Salkeld

1. From the church parking area turn left and then, opposite the Methodist Chapel, turn left up Outhwaite Road. Pass the church on the left beyond a beck. Soon the road turns right. Keep on along a stony track (which can be slippy on loose stones). Pass an information board which tells you about the Access Land of Black Fell. Soon you pass a barn on the left. At a point where there are fingerposts on each side of the track turn right to cross the (very difficult) stile signposted Beggars Trod/Haresceugh. Follow the wall on the left to reach and cross a ladder stile. Confronted by a wall turn right and follow it round a corner then keep following a fence on the left. At a fence junction turn right downhill slightly and cross a stile. Now keep on with a fence and then an old hawthorn field boundary above you on the left. Cross a stile by a wide field gate. Cross a little beck, and keep on a couple of yards to cross a stone stile (not waymarked) on the left into a walled plantation. Then turn right and follow a path (not very clear) inside and alongside the fence. Cross a stile and keep on to exit across another stile into a sloping field. Keep on with the fence on your right (follow an easy track) to come within sight of Outhwaite Farm. Go through a wide field gate on the right, and then turn left to walk past farm buildings and exit onto a gravel track near a fingerpost.

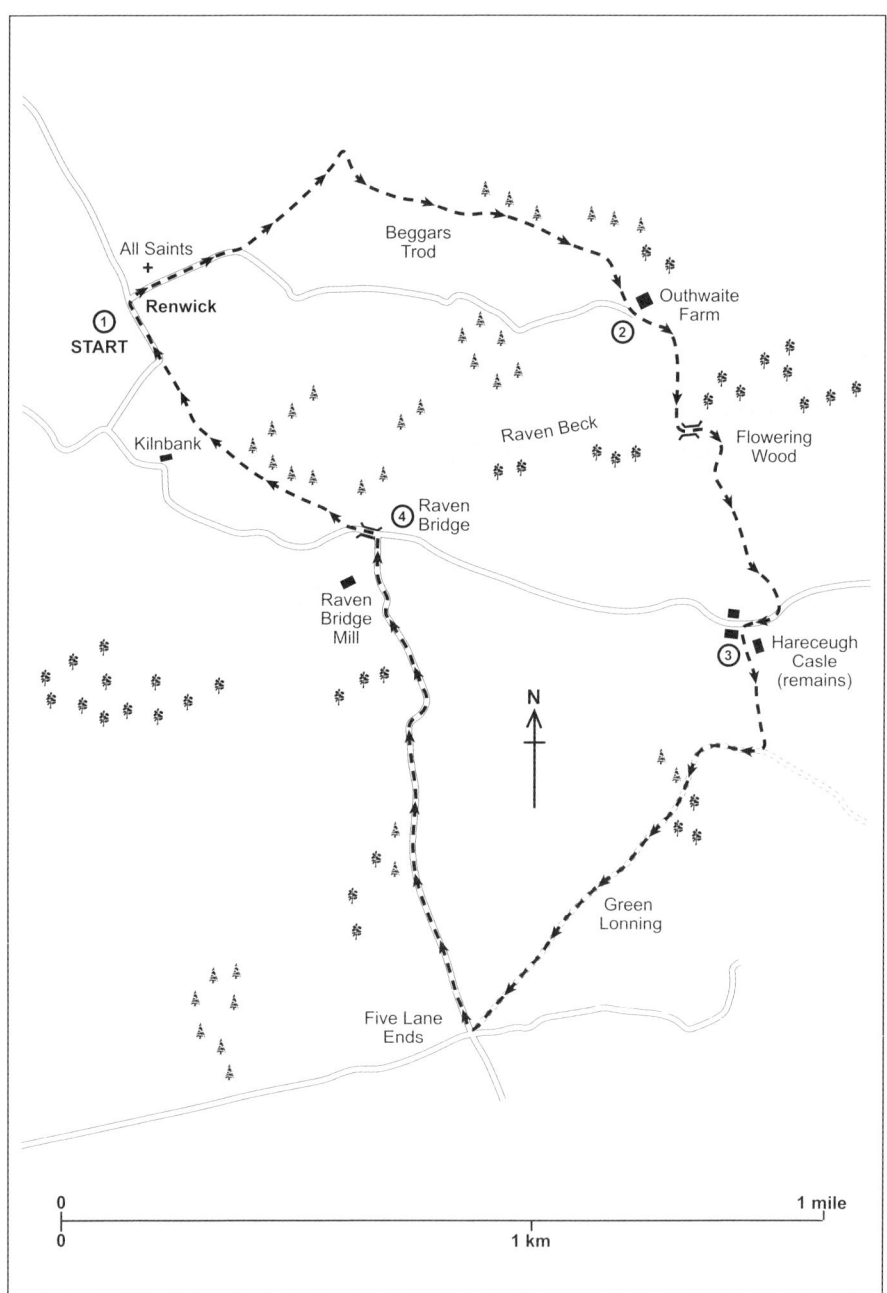

All Saints Church at Renwick. A peaceful scene now but a cockatrice once attacked builders here

> The Beggar's Trod runs from Brampton to Busk and is about 12 miles long. Tramps and itinerant workers used this route, begging food and shelter on the way. Outhwaite Farm is a typical hill farm with cows and sheep. The main danger to the sheep is their exposure to the biting Helm Wind blowing down the Pennines and resulting in weight loss as the sheep try to cope. The grass becomes bluish and dry and less nutricious. The Helm has been known to blow for nine days at a time.

2. Turn left and follow the track down through a wide gate and past the farmyard. Go on through a waymarked wide red gate, and then another just yards ahead. Now descend a green track with a beck down to the left (Raven Beck) and bank to the right. Where the track bends right – at a waymarked post – leave the track and go down the bank with care. At the bottom of the slope turn right and follow a fence round until you see a footbridge below you. Cross this then turn left into Flowering Wood (watch out for low hanging branches) to cross a partly hidden stile on the left. Follow the woodland path as it rises sharply then turns right. Exit over a good waymarked stile into a field. Turn right along the fence and then left

along a wall. Follow the wall on your right up to an enclosure. Pass to the left of this to exit via a wide field gate onto a road. Turn right along this to reach the hamlet of Haresceugh.

The cottage opposite the farm was once a pub. It stood on the old packhorse road to Alston. Haresceugh also stood on the old Via Regia or Monarch's Highway. This was the royal route around the kingdom and had to be maintained by local labour at a reasonable standard. The remains of Haresceugh Castle which you will pass are all that is left of a pele tower which guarded the Via Regia and was a place of safety during Border raids. It may also have been a watchtower to Kirkoswald Castle. The famous Haresceugh Luck discovered here, but now lost, was a drinking cup. It was eight inches in diameter and had a silver rim. Engraved on it were the words 'Should the bowl fall in feast or wassail farewell the luck of Haresceugh Castle'. Other 'lucks' have been found in Cumbria. There is a theory that they are linked to the legend of the Holy Grail.

3. Go through a wide field gate on the left marked public footpath to Busk. Follow a green track down over a ford then up to pass the remains of Haresceugh Castle on the left. Keep ahead through a field gate and on ahead with a wall to your right. Descend to the field corner and cross a difficult stile onto the Green Lonning. Turn right along this. At a complex junction (Five Lane Ends) turn right for Renwick.

4. Cross Raven Bridge and turn left at the junction. Within yards turn right up steps to a wicket gate (not signed). Go through then follow the right field edge fence. Go through a field gate then with the fence still to your right follow a grass track uphill past barns. Go through a field gate and then ahead to go through a double field gate. Head down the bank back into Renwick.

Ravenswick is the original name of Renwick ie. OE or Norse Hrafn or Raven. The name may be pre 800 AD. It was under Scottish control in 1086 and does not feature in Domesday Book. The manor was first created in the 12th century. A church is referred to in 1291. It was badly hit by Scots raids after 1314 then famine and the Black Death. It was on the route for the moving of silver from Alston to Carlisle. Before 1880 coal production was crucial to the village which had several pubs and also several blacksmiths to care for the horses which drew the coal wagons. By 1900 though it was simply reliant on agriculture and still has working farms in the village

The remains of Haresceugh Castle with Haresceugh in the background

itself. Oddly it has a long connection with Queen's College, Oxford which held the Lordship of the Manor from the 14th century through a bequest by the owner. Part of the manorial estate was Raven Bridge Mill (or Huddlesceugh Mill) where grain was ground until after the First World War. Tenants of the estate had to have their grain ground here and pay the Lord of the Manor a proportion of their flour. Further downstream is Renwick Mill

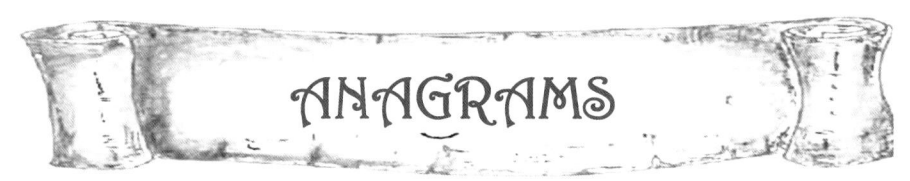

ANAGRAMS

These words have been mixed up.

Can you unscramble

lntetɡylra	basilisk
wrno	scalehouses
ikwrcɡn	renwick
dcsfgnoaifl	benedict
aibsslki	tallentyre
itcrɡacokc	church
bitdncɡɡ	rowan
oɡsaslɡcush	edgar
gradɡ	cockatrice
hcrhuc	scaffolding

WALK 10
MOREBATTLE AND KALE WATER

The only walk in the book involving any hill walking – but very modest. And uphill means good views – and downhill! You can also see indisputable proof of the existence of dragons – well almost!

THE LINTON WORM

During the twelfth century a monstrous worm tormented the good people of Linton and Morebattle in Roxburghshire on the Scottish borders.

In part it lived in the heart of Linton Loch – a small, boggy area and the ideal place for a monster to hide. Its other dark abode was a hollow on the north east side of Linton Hill.

Emerging from its lair at dusk and dawn to ravage the countryside, eating crops, livestock and people, it proved invulnerable to the weapons ranged against it. The landscape around the area became blackened, desolate and derelict and was avoided by the local population who were in fear of the Worm. Large rewards were offered in vain for the destruction of this monster, which had grown to so huge that it used to twist itself, in spiral folds, round a green hillock of considerable height. The hillock is now called Wormeston and marked by a clump of trees.

The story came to the ears of one John de Somerville of Lariston, a man brave even to acts of madness. He came to the village of Jedburgh where many of the country folk had fled, and heard many conflicting tales about the dragon. Some said the dragon was sprouting wings, and others said that the dragon had fiery venomous breath that could kill from afar.

He decided to go and see for himself. He rode close to the worm's lair and waited. In a short while the worm caught his scent, brought half of its body

Linton Worm

out of its lair, and stood gazing at him with its mouth hanging open, but did not attack. Observing the beast himself he saw that the creature would open its mouth wide to swallow anything in its path but when faced with something too large to eat would remain still, with its mouth open. Sensing an opportunity he went to a local blacksmith and had him forge an iron-covered spear with a point on which could be impaled a hunk of peat.

On the point of the lance he placed a burning peat turf, dowsed in pitch and brimstone. With this he practised riding in joust position, until his horse had become used to the acrid smoke blowing in its face. He then told the people of his intention to slay the dragon but was only scorned by the elders for his folly.

The next day at sunrise he went with a servant to the worm's lair. He sat on his horse in readiness, and when the beast lumbered forward from out of its cave the servant set fire to the peat. Somerville spurred his horse forward and in one swift movement shoved the burning peat into the worm's gaping maw. The aromatic quality of the peat is said to have preserved the champion from the effects of the monster's poisonous breath, while, at the same time, it clogged its jaws. In dying the serpent contracted its folds with so much violence, that their spiral impression is still discernible round the hillock where it lay.

The animal retreated to its lair to die, its thrashing tail bringing down the mountain around it and burying it forever.

Thus was delivered a fatal blow to the awesome Dragon of Linton.

Somerville's heroism was memorialised by a carved stone at Linton Kirk. He was made Royal Falconer, knighted and made 'First Barrone' of Linton. The crest of the Somervilles was a wyvern (heraldic dragon).

Today, both church and effigy still remain intact – and still provoke wonder, and perhaps even a little fear, in those that visit the little village of Linton.

NOTES
The Somervilles were a Norman family from the Caen area. Walter de Somerville fought at Hastings. He became Lord of Wicknor in Staffordshire and Aston Somerville in Gloucestershire. His two sons became founders of two lines of descent, one in England and one in Scotland. This was not unusual since King David I (1083-1153) followed a policy of granting land in Scotland to Norman families from England. The Scottish Somervilles became very wealthy and

powerful in a short space of time – which might lie partly behind the idea that they were elevated so quickly because of a physical deed. David also founded the burgh of Roxburgh which was one of the first founded in Scotland. A family history was written by James Somerville, 11th Lord Somerville in 1679. He related that William the Lion made John Somerville, his falconer, baron of Linton in Roxburghshire for killing a monstrous worm in 1174 – very precise of him. The title became dormant on the death of the 19th Lord Somerville in 1870.

The Orcadian folklorist Ernest Marwick highlights the similarity between the method used to kill the Linton Worm and those recounted in the slaying of the Stoor worm of the Orkneys, which was also killed with burning peat.

The area does have hilly topography but this is more likely due to the effects of glaciation rather than a writhing dragon. The little church stands on a hill of sand. Between it and Morebattle was once a marshy loch. The area did come to enjoy the name of 'wormington'. There is indeed a field where, it is claimed, was the Worm's Den although nowadays it is a scene of peaceful cultivation by unhurried natives.

However, most unusually for dragon and worm stories, there is pictorial evidence which dates back nearly to the time. There is a carved outline above the doorway of the church – the 'Somervail Stone' – which supposedly shows de Somerville's brave act. William Henderson commented on this in his 1879 book, *Notes on the Folk-lore of the Northern Counties of England and the Borders*. He wrote:

'A knight on horseback, clad in a tunic or hauberk, with a round helmet, urges his horse against two large animals, the foreparts of which only are visible, and plunges his lance into the throat of one. Behind him is the outline of another creature, apparently of a lamb. The heads of the monsters are strong and powerful, but more like those of quadrupeds than of serpents. It is perplexing also to see two of them, but not the less does popular tradition connect the representation with the Linton Worm.'

Henderson did not include in his description the fact that behind the knight's head is a bird, and in front of it what may have been a label with an inscription of six or possibly even seven letters.

The story and the carving fascinated Sir Walter Scott but he dismissed the latter:

'The sculpture itself gives no countenance to this fine story; for the animal, whom the knight appears to be in the act of slaying, has no resemblance to a serpent, but rather to a wolf, or boar, with which the neighbouring Cheviot mountains must in early times have abounded; and there remain vestiges of another monster, of the same species, attacking the horse of the champion.'
(*Minstrelsy of the Scottish Border, Vol. III*)

He did claim that there had once been an inscription as well of which he was told by the enthusiastic locals:

> The wode Laird of Lariestoun
> Slew the wode worm of Wormiestoune,
> And wan all Lintoan paroschine.

However this had been weathered away long ago. The carving on the tympanum or arch above the doorway does still remain though. It is Norman in origin and is unique in Scotland. Sadly attempts to protect it with perspex simply aggravated the erosion, but the covering has been removed now.

Reading between the lines you could see this as a *parvenu* foreign Norman family trying to justify themselves at a time when the novel feudal ownership of land was being established in Scotland.

THE WALK

What you need to know	
Distance	4.5 miles
Time	3.5 hours
Map	Ordnance Survey Explorer Outdoor Leisure 16 The Cheviot Hills
Starting point	From the little car park in front of St. Aidan's Church next to the Templehall Inn or roadside parking in Morebattle village centre. Grid Reference NT771249
Terrain	Mostly paths and tracks. There is a steep uphill gradient on the outward route but this is compensated for by a

Terrain cont'd	much longer descent, then easy riverside walking. There is road walking at the start but along quiet roads
How to get there	Morebattle stands on the B6401 near the junction with the B6436 from Kelso and is 5 miles west of Town Yetholm and 8.5 miles south of Kelso. Linton is on the B636 about a 1.5 miles north of Morebattle
Refreshments	The Templehall Inn and the little St. Cuthbert's Coffee Shop C.I.C at St. Aidan's Church. Postcode for SatNav: TD5 8QQ

1. From Morebattle head east along the main street following the signs for St. Cuthbert's Way (which will guide you constantly on the outward route). Just past the Old Police House at a road junction turn right (signed Hownam) and follow a single track road past the entrance to Corbett Tower and on to the next road junction. Turn right and follow this road alongside the Kale Water on for 350 yards past a ford on the left then turn left over a signed footbridge.

   Morebattle is a splendid name for a village in the once-disputed border area. The place-name comes from an Anglian phrase meaning 'dwelling place by the lake'. However Linton Loch between Morebattle and Linton was drained long ago. St. Aidan's Church is being restored. It is a 'Fresh Expression Church' used for a range of secular and religious activities. It has a small café. The village has a 'Teapot Street' which according to local legend was named by Sir Walter Scott, who, passing through the village one day, noticed the wives in the street carrying teapots to the nearby Kale Water to picnic, and remarked, "that must be Teapot Street".

2. Walk ahead a few yards to intersect a track across the middle of the field and then turn right to follow it as it turns and rises. Cross over a track and keep on following St. Cuthbert's Way uphill to an enclosed plantation. Cross a stile and keep on up the right side of this to go through a kissing gate onto open land. There are excellent views from this section. Now follow the clear path uphill. Beneath Grubbit Law it bends left and levels out. Before you reach a stone wall (or dyke) up the flank of Wideopen Hill you arrive at a distinct cross-tracks.

View from below Grubbit Law

St Cuthbert's Way is a 62-mile long-distance trail between Melrose and Holy Island. The walk is named after Cuthbert, a 7th century saint, a native of the Borders who spent his life in the service of the church. He began his work at Melrose Abbey. He achieved the status of Bishop, and when he died was buried on Holy Island. He was made a saint eleven years after his death, when his coffin was opened and his remains were found to be perfectly preserved.

3. Now turn left and begin to head downhill. You follow a wall on the right for some time. Follow the very clear stony tractor track down to go through a wide field gate then, across rough ground, resume the track on down along the left side of a wood, Grubbit Plantation. You arrive at a track junction with a wide gate on the right. Turn left here along the clear track. Turn right after a few yards and follow the track as it descends alongside the right edge of woodland towards a barn. Here it turns left and cuts through the wood and then right to follow the wood edge down to a track T-junction. Turn right here and follow this tractor track steadily on across

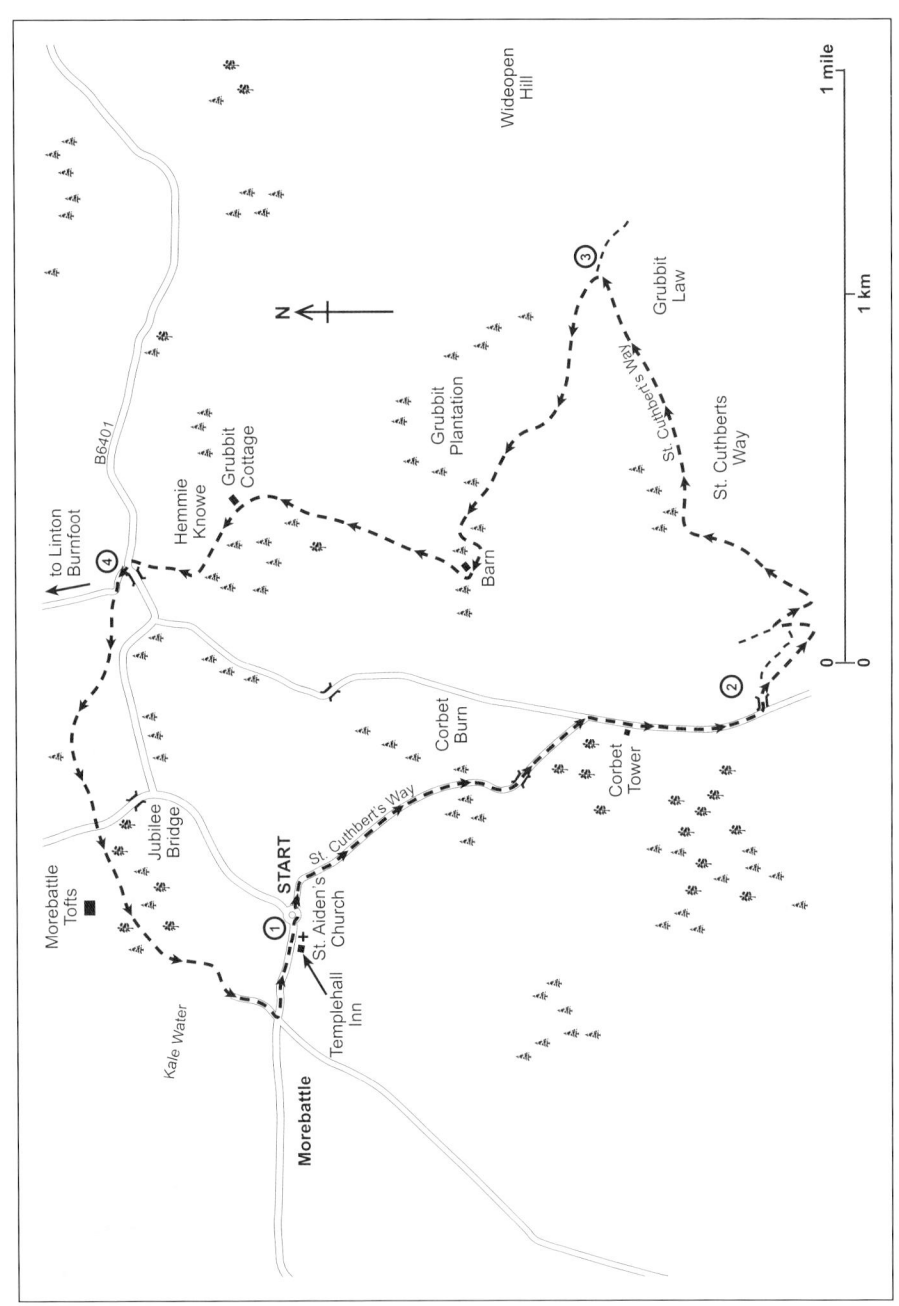

Linton Church stands on a sandy mound which was once surrounded by water and marshland

fields and over cattle grids with woodland over on the left. It turns left past Grubbit Cottage and continues over cattle grids to reach a road (B6401) near a hump backed bridge.

4. Cross over the road to walk a few yards up a minor road (to Linton Burnfoot). At the first bend turn left on a path through a field gate. Now keep on alongside the Kale Water. At an open field cross over diagonally right to go through a wicket gate near a finger-post onto a road (B6436) near cottages, with the Jubilee Bridge a few yards on the left. Cross the road to follow a farm drive for a few yards then immediately go left through a kissing gate into a field. Follow a grassy path diagonally right towards another kissing gate next to the river bank. Follow the riverside woodland path on to an

The rather grand Linton Manse near the church

View from Linton Church towards the Cheviots

iron footbridge. Cross the bridge. Follow the grassy path as it rises uphill to the right to reach a kissing gate and stile. Go through and down a path then turn left along a lane to exit onto the main road through Morebattle.

A mile and a half to the north of Morebattle lies the hamlet of Linton. Standing there on a sandy mound which was once surrounded by water and marshland is Linton Church. The mound has been a site of worship for over 850 years. It contains a Norman font. The chancel stalls are carved from 17th century oak and marked with the arms of ruling families. Outside there is a two sided sundial dated 1699 in the south west corner. The gem of the church though is the 'Somervail Stone' above the porch door showing a knight fighting two beasts. This Norman stone is unique in Scotland. Opposite the church is the impressive manse. The Jubilee Bridge at Morebattle was built to commemorate Queen Victoria's jubilee in 1887.

WORD SEARCH

r	w	u	n	f	e	a	q	l	e	y	l	w	o	e
p	q	w	b	y	l	i	t	w	k	j	y	p	n	r
d	e	s	y	t	l	n	r	i	h	v	h	o	n	c
a	h	j	d	m	i	i	e	i	e	d	t	r	o	l
b	j	m	w	k	v	v	n	r	a	s	x	k	r	n
e	q	l	d	m	r	m	n	t	m	l	v	m	m	k
g	l	f	j	q	e	v	v	i	o	w	p	d	a	m
p	o	t	m	o	m	h	r	x	o	n	l	r	n	r
b	l	x	t	c	o	b	p	v	b	e	c	h	c	o
z	c	m	d	a	s	m	o	n	s	t	e	r	b	w
i	o	x	e	d	b	s	s	z	g	f	b	y	r	i
y	u	v	y	w	w	e	f	c	v	a	w	w	q	p
m	m	p	n	o	v	e	r	d	e	s	r	o	h	v
y	g	s	z	b	h	o	r	o	q	c	h	q	r	j
h	e	p	d	o	x	z	t	s	m	p	q	s	e	n

brimstone

horse

lair

linton

monster

morebattle

norman

somerville

worm

wyvern

RECOMMENDED READING

All serious scholarly works must have a bibliography so here goes!

Green, Roger Lancelyn *The Book of Dragons* (Penguin, 1973). A delightful compendium of dragon stories 'for those of eight and over'.

Grice, Frederick *Folk Tales of the North Country* (Nelson, 1944). Long out of print but an invaluable source for serious dragon hunters of the north east.

Griffiths, Bill *Meet the Dragon* (Heart of Albion, 1996). A very thorough and readable account of the origin of dragon stories.

Henderson, Joan *The Laidley Worm of Bamborough* (Newcastle City Libraries, 1991). Delightfully illustrated. The basic story.

Henderson, Joan *The Lambton Worm* (Newcastle City Libraries). Beautiful clear illustrations. The basic and most popular account of the most famous northern dragon.

Loftmark, Carl *A History of the Red Dragon* (Welsh Heritage Series, 1995). Addresses the story of the Welsh dragon and dragons in general.

Manning-Sanders, Ruth *A Book of Dragons* (Methuen, 1964). 'Not all dragons want to gobble up princesses' of course. This is a compendium of dragon stories from all over the world.

Telfer, Paul *The Legend of the Sockburn Worm* (Iron Chest, 1991). Thorough coverage of the story and various aspects of it.

Walker, Peter *Folk Tales from the North York Moors* (Robert Hale, 1990). Excellent coverage of the leading dragon stories of the North Yorkshire Moors.

Westwood, Jennifer *Albion: a Guide to Legendary Britain* (Paladin, 1987). As the title suggests this is concerned with the much wider world of legends and folklore in Britain.

Wharton, Violet et alia *Dragons and Fabulous Beasts* (Pavilion, 1994). A very attractive little illustrated collection of fabulous animals.

Whitlock, Ralph *Here Be Dragons* (Allen and Unwin, 1983). The definitive gazetteer of dragons.

WEBSITES
www.mysteriousbritain.co.uk

More books from Sigma Press

Discover Northumberland Volume 3
30 coastal and inland walks
Mark Lejk

This is the third volume of Discover Northumberland and contains 30 circular walks covering the whole of Northumberland. It is aimed at people of all walking abilities and preferences with lengths ranging from 2.1 km (1.3 miles) Many of the longer walks have shorter versions and altogether the different variations and combinations make 50 routes. The walks range from the far north of the county on the Scottish border to the southern border with County Durham visiting the fabulous Northumberland coastline and the wonderful countryside inland along the way. Some of the walks are Northumberland classics but many are new, being specially created by the author after a lot of research and exploration. All the walks have detailed directions and a map and have been personally tracked by the author. They are supplemented with interesting commentaries about the places visited along the way.
£9.99

Discover Northumberland
Hadrian's Wall Country
Mark Lejk

30 circular walks covering the whole of Northumberland from north to south and east to west aimed at people of all walking abilities and preferences with lengths ranging from 4.5 km (2.8 miles) to 17.8 km (11.1 miles) and difficulty ranging from easy to strenuous. Many of the longer walks have shorter versions and altogether the different variations and combinations make for 48 routes.
£9.99

Discover Northumberland Volume 2
30 coastal and inland walks
Mark Lejk

This is the second volume of *Discover Northumberland* and contains another 30 circular walks covering the whole of Northumberland. It is aimed at people of all walking abilities and preferences with lengths ranging from 1.6 km (1 mile) to 22.3 km (13.9 miles) and difficulty ranging from easy to strenuous. Many of the longer walks have shorter versions and altogether the different variations and combinations make 46 routes. Some of the walks are classics but many are new, being specially created by the author after a lot of research and exploration.
£9.99

A Walker's Guide to the History of Northumberland
Andrew Lowes

Northumberland boasts a huge diversity in the character of its landscape. From the wild uplands of the Cheviot Hills and North Pennines, to the fertile valleys of the Tyne and Tweed and on to the magnificent cliffs and sweeping beaches of the coastal fringe, the county has almost everything. The history is very special too, with some of the most influential events in British history having happened here. Stone, Bronze and Iron Age people, Romans, Dark Age Warlords and Christians, Reivers and Industrialists have all left their mark. It's all there to be discovered if you know where to look.
£9.99

A Walker's Guide to the Border Reivers
Andrew Lowes

Today the Anglo-Scottish Border is a tranquil and beautiful place. But it hasn't always been this way, between the 11th and 16th centuries it was a lawless frontline between two rival and insecure kingdoms. The 28 walks take the reader through the wild borderlands and trails used by the reiver to spirit away stolen cattle, into the lairs of the most feared villains and to some of the 200 or so fortified buildings that remain. This book provides a fascinating insight into the world of the Borderers in our not so distant past.
£9.99

Northumberland Walks
You Take the High Road
with alternative routes to suit all abilities
Anne Leuchars & Debby Waldron
Together they have devised walks which bring equal pleasure to both types of walker. Each walk splits into harder sections for fitter people and easier tracks for slower walkers. In most cases you all set off together, then separate part way through and meet up again to complete the walk together. The walks also accommodate differences in approach to a day in the countryside. Some people like the satisfaction of several miles or a steep hill conquered, others prefer to stroll along, taking rests along the way to relish the views.
£8.99

All-Terrain Pushchair Walks
The North York Moors
Zoë Sayer and Rebecca Terry
'All-Terrain' means just that - suitable for all forms of landscape - and experienced authors and walkers Rebecca and Zoë have chosen the North York Moors for the latest in this popular series of 'All-Terrain Pushchair Walks'. Cchoose from strolls along the riverside, rambles through heather moors or walks by the sea on secluded beaches and breathtaking cliffs. The park has a well-established extensive network of paths and bridleways, and Rebecca and Zoë have used this existing network to plan these thirty pushchair-friendly walks, but they have made sure that before you set out with your pushchair you'll know exactly what to expect.
£8.99

River Tyne Trail: sources to sea
Peter Donaghy & Peter Laidler
The stone at the North Tyne, near the England-Scotland border, was erected in October 2013 specially to mark the beginning of the trail. From tiny springs to streams and then vibrant rivers, the two sources eventually converge to create the powerful River Tyne as it journeys to the sea. The nature of the undulating terrain makes for a challenging and rewarding experience as the trail passes through some of Britain's most beautiful and interesting scenery. This book is the brainchild of former businessman Brian Burnie, the founder of the Cancer Patient Care Charity 'Daft as a Brush'. Brian hopes that this walk will promote the work of the charity which provides individualised transport for patients requiring cancer treatment.
£12.99

Northumbria Walks with Children
Stephen Rickerby
Over 20 walks are included covering the North East from the Tees to the Tweed. There are questions (with answers!) and checklists to both challenge and interest the children, as well as practical information for parents. All walks are less than 5 miles long, exploring the great variety of scenery and heritage of Northumbria.
'This is a splendid collection that will excite and stimulate youngsters.'
– Sunderland Echo

£8.99

Northumberland Place Names
Anthony Poulton-Smith

Some of the definitions give a glimpse of life in the earlier days of the settlement, and for the author there is nothing more satisfying than finding a name which gives such a snapshot. The definitions are supported by anecdotal evidence, bring to life the individuals and events which have influenced the places and how these names have developed. This is not simply a dictionary but a history and will prove invaluable not only for those who live and work in the county but also visitors and tourists, historians and former inhabitants, indeed anyone with an interest in Northumberland and the city of Newcastle upon Tyne.
£8.99

County Durham Place Names
Anthony Poulton-Smith

Some of the definitions give a glimpse of life in the earlier days of the settlement, and for the author there is nothing more satisfying than finding a name which gives such a snapshot. The definitions are supported by anecdotal evidence, bring to life the individuals and events which have influenced the places and how these names have developed.

This is not simply a dictionary but a history and will prove invaluable not only for those who live and work in the county but also visitors and tourists, historians and former inhabitants, indeed anyone with an interest in County Durham.
£8.99

Walking the Cheviots
Classic Circular Routes
Edward Baker
This book provides an excellent introduction to this solitary, wild countryside. Everyone is catered for from weekend family walkers to the experienced hill walker with all the walks personally checked and trod by the author. Each route contains details of the natural history, geology and archaeology of the area descriptively written by Edward Baker who has lived his whole life in the region. For ease of reference, the book is in two sections, covering the northern and southern Cheviots – distinct areas with their own unique character. There are almost 50 walks – by far the most comprehensive collection published for the Cheviots.
£9.99

Coast to Coast
On the Ravenber Way
Ron Scholes
The walk described in the book follows existing rights of way in the form of footpaths, bridleways and tracks, making this cross-country route a challenging long-distance journey. The walk commences at Ravenglass, it passes Lakeland's finest array of high peaks, climbs over the high Pennines, traverses the northern moors and ends at Berwick-upon-Tweed.
£8.99

The Clough Walk from Nottingham to Sunderland
Martin Perry & Geoff Smith
The Clough Walk is a beautiful, exhilarating long distance walk that passes through the towns and cities associated with the illustrious career of Brian Clough, both as a player and manager. The walk begins in Nottingham and ends on the impressive North East coast on Roker Beach, Sunderland and affords the walker the opportunity to visit football grounds and various memorial sites and statues along the way.
£8.99

Walking The Northumberland Dales
Hadrian's Wall Country
Jennifer Norderhaug & Barbara Thompson
Discover and explore the lesser-known landscapes of the Northumberland Dales – a land of far horizons and secret corners. The book includes routes in North and South Tynedale, Allendale, Hexhamshire, Blanchland and Hadrian's Wall, and routes within easy access of Newcastle-upon-Tyne, Durham and other popular locations – with forays into Cumbria and County Durham. It features 28 medium grade, cross-country walks offering variety and choice away from the tourist trail. It is packed with interest on the history, industrial archaeology, geography and the traditions and culture of the area.
£8.95

North York Moors
circular cycle rides
David Branson

A 135 miles circular cycling route around the North York Moors, using off road tracks and minor roads, with fascinating information on the many interesting places en-route. The trip is both an exhilarating experience and voyage of discovery in an area crammed with breathtaking scenery and enchanting places of interest.
£8.99

Yorkshire Dales Trigpointing Walks
Hill walking with a point to it!
Keith Stevens

This book introduces the pastime of trigpointing, with 25 walks in the Yorkshire Dales, each aimed at finding Ordnance Survey pillars. They're just pyramids of stone, nothing to right home about, but they're part of our heritage and worthy of our patronage. It's an excuse to get out in the fresh air and try out some new ground, with the objective of reaching the pillars adding a new dimension to the walking experience.
£9.99

Adventure Walks for Little Explorers
in the Yorkshire Dales
Rebecca Chippindale and Rebecca Terry
This isn't just a book of fifteen walks for small children – it's an all-inclusive family adventure. Grab your 'Kit' and prepare to open up your senses. Feel parts of the journey, magnify the Yorkshire Dales, collect items along the way and create something different when you get home.
£8.99

All of our books are available through booksellers.
For a free catalogue, please contact:

Sigma Leisure, Stobart House, Pontyclerc Penybanc Road, Ammanford SA18 3HP
Tel: 01269 593100
info@sigmapress.co.uk   www.sigmapress.co.uk